Worship & Y...

F4416

Worship
& Youth Culture

A guide to alternative worship

BY

PETE WARD

MarshallPickering
An Imprint of HarperCollins*Publishers*

Marshall Pickering is an imprint of
HarperCollins*Religious*
Part of HarperCollins*Publishers*
77–85 Fulham Palace Road, London W6 8JB

First published in Great Britain
in 1993 by Marshall Pickering

10 9 8 7 6 5 4 3 2 1

The author and illustrator assert the moral right to be
identified as the author and illustrator of this work

A catalogue record for this book is
available from the British Library

ISBN 0 551 02658-8

Printed and bound in Great Britain by
HarperCollinsManufacturing Glasgow

Conditions of Sale

To JOY

Contents

Acknowledgements

This book is largely a corporate effort. Many of the practical ideas for worship have arisen from the joint creativity of all the people in our worship service, JOY. It has been a privilege to be able to be a part of such an exciting and inspiring group. This book is really JOY's.

Nevertheless, since writing this book JOY has changed and evolved. A new leadership group has taken over – while I now concentrate on outreach to young people with Oxford Youth Works. If you like, what we have here is a snapshot representing our first year together (summer 1991 to summer 1992).

But the people who make up JOY have not just been an inspiration to me to put pen to paper. Their faith in God and their commitment to each other have challenged me to look again at my life, and for that I must thank them. I would also like to take this occasion to thank those in St Mary and John Church and St Aldate's Church who have supported the JOY service, in particular Fr Martin Flatman, Debbie Lake, and the Rev. David MacInnes.

Thanks are also due to those who have given me quotes and suggestions as I have put this book together. Tom, Andy, Wilson and Stu deserve special mention for being willing to have their spiritual experiences retold. Those who read the book as it was in the making – wonderful people – include Simon and Anna Hall, Crispin Fletcher, Father Martin, Sam Adams, Tess Ward, Tim Dakin and Mary Louis. I also want to say a big thank you to Christine Smith for all the advice and comments which helped me to get this book into shape.

Writing a book is an antisocial habit and I want to say thank you to my wife, Tess, for being willing to put up with a possessed monster who rabbits on about his book all the time! I am grateful for her patience over the last few months.

Pete Ward
Oxford 1992

Part One

Thinking about Worship

1 · Something New Is Happening

Yesterday the phone rang. "I hear you have started an Alternative Worship Service. We're just about to do the same in our area – can you help us?" said the voice on the other end of the line.

This sort of request is not unusual. In fact, I have been surprised how many people want to know about new ways for young people to worship. There seems to have been a sudden significant movement in the life of the Church. Most people know about St Thomas Crookes and the Nine O'Clock Service in Sheffield, some have heard of Holy Joe's in London or even of our own service in Oxford called JOY.

Here and elsewhere around the country people are starting to explore a fresh approach to worship. A key feature of this movement is the way youth culture has been used as a creative part of what happens in the service. A multi-media approach to worship is beginning to develop. Dance music and live rock bands are appearing in services as well as video and visual images. This diverse approach to worshipping God is immensely exciting and stimulating. No wonder so many people are interested in alternative worship.

Getting going

As people see what God is doing in these places, some are thinking that something similar could happen in their own area. But how do you get an alternative worship service started?

The amazing multi-media worship services that some churches are developing can appear daunting, if not impossible, to re-create in your own church. If this is how you feel then this book aims to be exactly what the doctor ordered for you.

Over the last year in Oxford I have been involved with the setting up and developing of an alternative worship service. This book is based on our experience, but it is also a guide for anyone who wants to see young people expressing themselves in worship. It can be helpful to hear how others went about something – not because you want to copy them, but because their story might help you develop your own ideas. In describing JOY I don't want to make any great claims for what we have done. But this book is based on a belief that given the necessary call of God and help from the Spirit alternative worship could evolve in many different places and churches.

Yet I do not want to give the false impression that this sort of thing can happen overnight. Real alternative worship needs to grow slowly. It needs to be nurtured and encouraged over a period of time. Even more challenging, alternative worship does not start inside the church, but *outside*.

Starting with the outsiders

Alternative worship is created when young people are set free to express their faith in their own cultural terms. It is tempting to think that merely setting up a new kind of service in our church will attract large numbers of young people. But this is a bit too easy. Many people I talk with are interested in this new style of worship because they think it will help their church youth group. This may well be the case, but if you build your service entirely around young people who to some extent already share church culture, you will not create a genuine alternative.

Real alternative worship will only be created by young people who are culturally and socially outside the Church. It is their culture which makes it truly "alternative". It will reflect their ways of speaking and relating, and of course their kinds of music.

We also need to realize that Christian adults cannot provide alternative worship for young people. We can't lay on a service and expect that young people outside the Church will come along to it. This approach is not really "alternative" – it's just a variation on what we already do in Church. If we think we should provide alternative worship for young people, then we have missed the point. We can't create this kind of worship *for* young people. We have to create it *with* them.

This means that we need to have established some kind of real contact with groups of young people who live in our local area. I'm not talking here about young people who already come to church or have been brought up in Christian homes. I'm talking about those who are at present outside of the Church. If we want to see our churches renewed by genuinely alternative worship, then we need to be prepared to start with these young people.

The life, energy and creativity which can transform the Church are readily available. All around us there are groups of young people whose daily lives reflect this fact. They listen to new and challenging types of music, they are acutely aware of changes in fashion, and the way things look is of utmost importance to them. They are in touch with issues like the environment, homelessness and unemployment because they experience these things at the sharp end of life. If we want to see alternative worship become a living reality, we must be willing to make the journey outside of our Church culture and environment into their world. We need their help to bring new life into our worship. It is their music, energy and vision for life empowered by the Spirit of God which will make our Church into something which is truly alternative. This sort of journey is a kind of missionary endeavour.

Mission is reaching out in friendship

Alternative worship has its roots in long-term mission work amongst groups of young people. In Oxford our own service has grown from the patient work of a team of about twenty Christian adults spending time building friendships with local young people. It took about eight years of hard graft before we were ready to start our own church service. Just like missionaries we had to be willing to spend time with young people so that we could learn their language, feel their concerns, share their joys and their problems. More importantly, we had to be willing to stick around long enough to become trusted as their friends. It is only through this kind of long-term friendship that those currently outside the life of the Church will ever come to know the Good News about Jesus.

I have already written in *Youth Culture and the Gospel* about the need for Christian adults to build relationships with groups of non-Christian young people. These relationships need to come before any kind of alternative worship service precisely because it is the young people and the culture they inhabit which actually form the worship. To start with the worship and then hope to attract the young people is to put the cart before the horse!

To begin with young people who are currently outside the Church means that we start off with evangelism. If you want some ideas on how to go about sharing the Good News of Jesus with local young people, I refer you to *Youth Culture and the Gospel*. But if we want to share the Gospel with young people outside the cultural framework of the Church, we need to be able to express the truth about Jesus in ways which they can relate to. They need to see in concrete ways how being a Christian will make sense in their cultural environment. We need to be willing not only to live out the Christian life in front of them, but also to re-express the truth about Jesus in terms which they can understand. It is when young people respond to a Jesus who makes sense in their cultural world that alternative worship is born.

Worship in its simplest form is an honest response to the free gift of life that Jesus offers us. When young people respond to Jesus, that is worship. But when they reach out to Jesus from within their cultural world, using their own language and expressions, something new and exciting is created. This kind of worship is truly "alternative" because it grows from their culture.

Jesus said the Kingdom of God is like a mustard seed. Alternative worship may have a small beginning, but it holds the potential for amazing growth and development. The image of planting a seed is powerful because it speaks of the important steps that must happen before a service can be set up.

The mustard seed approach to alternative worship

To grow alternative worship from small beginnings, before anything gets off the ground in church, we need to:

1. get to meet young people and form friendships with them
   – a slow, sacrificial and time-consuming process
2. gain the trust of the group
3. learn to share our faith in terms that they can understand and relate to
4. start to help them develop their own authentic style of worship and praise

If we want to see large bushes and trees growing, this is where seed planters need to put their time and energy.

New growth

Over the last eight or nine years at Oxford Youth Works we have been putting these ideas into practice. During this time many young people have become Christians but unfortunately very few of them have ever found a long-term home in a local church.

It was probably inevitable that these young people would not feel comfortable inside a church. The problem with sharing the Gospel as a seed which then grows in a new cultural

environment is that once it starts to grow, it is very difficult
to transplant. The young people we took along to church found
it very hard to fit in. They didn't like the music or the lack of
opportunity for open discussion. They especially didn't like
the male dominated, upfront role of many of the preachers or
ministers. The formal nature of many church services was hard
for them to cope with, and an hour without a fag was too much
for some to bear! The culture of these churches was also alien
to them as it didn't seem to reflect their concerns, experiences
or interests.

We had been holding our own weekly informal teaching and
worship session for some time. We encouraged the young
people to be extremely creative in these times. They wrote their
own songs expressing their experience of God, they would get
into groups and discuss Bible passages and they would maybe
respond to the Bible reading by creating a piece of art or drama.
In all these ways we tried to encourage the young people to
develop their own approach to the Christian faith. We fed and
watered the seed in their lives.

What we did not do was try to shape the growth of this new
plant. We adopted this approach deliberately because we
realized that they needed to remain in contact with their own
local communities and friendship networks. Making them
conform to our cultural norms would separate them from their
roots.

One of the problems with introducing young people to a local
church is that as they grow in their faith they almost inevitably
take on its middle-class values and attitudes. It's almost as if
Jesus and the prevailing culture within our churches are so
inextricably intermixed that we have ceased to recognize which
is which. Young people from a working-class background who
join a church find it difficult to stay in touch with their friends
or in some cases even their own families. The middle-class
culture of the church is very powerful. This is precisely the
reason why so many young people find it hard to join a church
in the first place.

In helping our group of young people to explore the faith for themselves apart from the church, we saw something genuinely new and exciting starting to take shape. This approach to living the Christian life was really alternative worship. The problem was: How was it going to last?

Time for Church

We soon found that the young people who came to our various discipleship groups were starting to drift away. They needed something a bit more meaty, which challenged them to live out their faith in new ways and demanded much more of them in terms of commitment. In brief they needed Church. But none of them had really found a place in the established churches around. It was at this point that the idea of JOY was born.

If the local churches did not have anything to which young people could relate, we began to ask ourselves whether we should approach them and offer to start something. Our aim was not to change an already existing service or congregation and try to make it ''alternative''. What we wanted was a time slot when the church building was not being used. In an empty church we could create our own type of service. We did not want to impose JOY type worship on the regular church-goers. In a separate time slot we could feel free to do what we wanted without stepping on the toes of people who had grown up with the traditional type of church service. With our own service we could focus on the needs of young people. In time, however, some of the local congregation started to come to our services and some of the JOY people started to go to the regular Sunday morning service.

One point of contact with the local church was through a group of students in St Aldate's Church who were already experimenting with Rave Worship. Some of them had started to get to know our young people. In fact they had been coming along to our discipleship group (which we call Worship) and had helped us on a couple of occasions by running secular raves which had gone down well. The students and our young people made a total of about 25, enough to consider starting a regular worship service.

We were helped further by an invitation from the Greenbelt Festival to run an Alternative Communion Service. During the summer of 1991 the students and young people started to plan this service. The young people were mostly musicians who formed a band which performed in the local pubs in Oxford. They started to write music which could be used in the Communion service, including their own versions of a number of the responses found in the Anglican liturgy. The students for their part included a DJ and some talented artists who could work on visual images which we could project as slides. Planning the service and then going away to Greenbelt together helped these two very different groups to get to know each other. By the end of the festival it was clear that there was enough energy in this united group to make a start on planning a more regular service in a local church.

Making a home in a church

Despite the link with St Aldate's Church we did not end up worshipping in their building. During the build-up to Greenbelt we had held a rehearsal service in St Mary and John Church in east Oxford. This church is close to the area where most of the young people came from and it is much less of a student church than St Aldate's. It had no Sunday evening service so we had plenty of time to set up our gear. The church was also very high in its tradition – all smells and bells, as they say. Many of us in JOY are from an evangelical background, so the chance to interact with an Anglo-Catholic style of worship was very interesting. The parish priest of St Mary and John is also very much involved with the charismatic movement which created a common bond with St Aldate's, and also opened a door to explore this side of worship as well.

In October 1991 JOY started to run two services a month on Sunday evenings at 9pm. We also held smaller fellowship groups and worship sessions, some during the week and others on a Sunday. In addition people met to plan the services and in a large group to make decisions. Chapters 7 and 8 give more details on how we organized ourselves.

Our first service at St Mary and John was extremely exciting. We arrived at the church in the afternoon and the first job was to move most of the chairs out of the centre of the church. St Mary and John is an old Victorian church with stained glass windows, large stone pillars, and lots of nineteenth-century religious statues. Luckily the seats are all movable so we could create our own space inside this very atmospheric building.

From the pillars we suspended large sheets to create a smaller square-shaped worship area, and we projected massive images onto these sheets. One was a psychedelic picture of Jesus, another portrayed an angel all in blue. It made a highly visual and very exciting space for the worship.

Next we set up a sound system for the DJ and the young people set up the equipment for their band. In one corner we placed the altar and covered it in our own psychedelic cloth. Candles burned all around the altar.

Before the service started we played dance music very loud and the congregation either sat on the floor or stood around chatting. A few people started to dance in small groups. The service started with the band playing, again very loud, with lyrics projected on a screen so people could join in when they got the hang of it. The whole service was led by young people, including the prayers and the sermon. When we came to the Communion, the priest, Father Martin, dressed in all his robes chanted the words of consecration over the top of a dance track. Then all the congregation slowly filed forward to receive Communion as more dance music was played. The whole service took less than fifty minutes. It was an unforgettable occasion.

2 · Meeting God in Worship

A couple of months ago I was sitting with a bunch of young people in an old church. The building was in darkness apart from a single lit candle which centred our attention on a stone altar with a cross on it. The young people were quietly singing songs accompanied by a guitar. After a short reading from the Bible and some time for thinking their own thoughts, the group was invited to pray.

They were each asked to clench their fists and then to think about their lives in relation to God. They were then invited in a very gentle and sensitive way to open up their lives to God. Their fists could symbolize what they were thinking, opened out or closed tight to shut God out. Music was played while people responded to God in the way they felt was right for them.

What happened during this time of prayer was extraordinary. God's Spirit began to touch the young people in profound ways. It is hard to describe exactly what this experience was like. It was as if God's presence with us was so strong you could reach out and touch him. Of course that is what many of these young people were doing. The occasion is deeply imprinted in my mind and I can still recall the sense of awe. The whole group was coming close to the mystery and wonder of God.

But for me what was so exciting about this time of prayer and worship was that most of the young people involved were not Christians. In fact a good many of them came from very tough working-class backgrounds with very little previous contact with the Christian faith. This was the first time they had ever reached out to God in prayer.

Evangelism and worship

I'm sharing this experience of God with you because it opens up the whole question of how worship and evangelism should relate to each other. In most Christian youth work the experience of worship is to some extent detached from the process of evangelism. We set up a two-stage process. We preach the Gospel and then, if the young people are interested, we invite them along to a church to experience worship. In many ways this approach to evangelism is forced upon us by the fact that most young people find church very difficult. So we manufacture ways to share the Gospel which are outside the regular worshipping life of the church. We plan coffee bars or rock concerts or theatre shows because we know that non-Christian young people, on the whole, will not come to a church to hear about Jesus.

The problem with these sorts of events is that they lack the element of worship. Of course at a rock concert or even at a coffee bar young people can hear about Jesus, but it is very difficult to create space where they can start to open up to God in worship. This is a real drawback, for while we need to be very sensitive in introducing young people to the experience of worship, so much energy and power seem to flow from God when we get this sort of thing right. Some space for worship in response to a very simple explanation of the Good News of Jesus should be a much more frequent part of our youth work practice.

Young people need to experience the presence of God for themselves. This is particularly true for those who come from a working-class background. Of course the first evidence of God's presence with them will probably be their friendship with a Christian adult. This sort of relationship can demonstrate to a young person exactly how the Christian life works out in practice in their local area. But there is also the need for time and space to be given over to worship. Our experience has been that most young people whom we have seen come to faith point back to a time of worship as the turning point in their lives.

Some people may feel that to place so much emphasis on worship is a bit dodgy. I am recommending an approach to evangelism that is based heavily on a sense of the presence of God. I am talking about conversion as an experience of Jesus as a person who is alive today. This emphasis I believe is extremely important because it corrects the view that the Gospel is only a set of ideas to which we assent. Certainly, some preaching or teaching is necessary for real evangelism to take place, for each one of us is a mixture of feelings and intellectual thought. But it seems to me that the Good News of Jesus can be presented at both the intellectual and the emotional levels and that both are equally valid. What is important is that we don't get one out of balance with the other.

We do, however, need to accept the fact that within the world of young people experience rather than intellectual consideration is most likely to predominate. In fact one could say that youth culture is based on a collection of different kinds of experiences. Young people are interested in what feels good and they go to great lengths to achieve what is often a short-lived and shallow experience. But the Christian faith also has an experiential aspect to it and one which has a great deal to offer to young people. This experiential aspect of Christianity is most frequently seen in the presence of God amongst us when we worship.

Experiencing God

Creating spaces for young people to experience God in worship can be very tricky. On a number of occasions I have misjudged the feel of a particular group and the whole thing has backfired. But if you have already built up a trusting relationship then given some thought and careful planning it is possible.

The small worship service I have already described took place in a church late at night on a Saturday after we had spent the whole day together doing fun type activities. But the group had already experienced a similar worship time on our annual holiday. This holiday is designed specifically for non-Christian young people and each day we explain a little bit about the life and ministry of Jesus. Towards the end of the week we invite anyone who wants to know more about Jesus to come to a worship session. Over the years a number of young people have become Christians through this holiday. Interestingly enough worship has often been the starting point of their journey of faith. The worship service on the last night, many say, was one of the most important factors in their eventual conversion to Christ.

The worship service is very simple. We all bundle into a small room lit by a number of candles. Young people are sprawled out all over the place, on the floor, in each other's arms, sitting, lying, in fact generally anything which feels comfortable is okay. The service centres around a few simple songs which young people themselves have written over the years. After the singing we usually spend some time in silence when they are invited to ask God to be near them and to touch them. We explain that if they want to meet God he is holding out his arms to them and promises to come to them. They don't have to say any special words, they just need to be willing to be quiet and make some space for God.

After a time of silence one person will read a passage from the Bible. My favourite is Isaiah 55 where God invites his people to come to him and be fed: "Why spend money on what does not satisfy?" (v2) he says. "Come to me and you will have life."

This service is always very special and full of God's presence. You can feel God's delight at being invited into these young people's lives for the first time. During the week they have heard about Jesus, and they have been invited to follow him if they want to, but it is invariably during worship that Jesus meets them.

In their own words

Andy, Tom and Wilson, who were involved in the holiday and the worship service a few years ago, described to me how important worship can be in the process of conversion. Their experiences also demonstrate how worship which grows from young people opening up to God can be extremely refreshing and innovative. Young people like these will be our teachers and our guides as we set up alternative worship services in church. Here's what Andy had to say about his first experience of worship.

"It was awesome, I was gob-smacked, I was sat in an uncomfortable position and I could hardly walk when I got up, but I never noticed it. The experience touched me deep inside, it was meaningful, it felt comfortable, like carefree and yet not carefree, problems didn't get pushed to the back of your mind, they just didn't seem to matter. It was the major step towards me becoming a Christian, as if something was there, I knew that God had touched me. In the worship there was some Spirit there, one minute it wasn't there and then it was. During the week we had been asked to accept God but this was like a role reversal, God accepted us into himself. The Spirit was there with open arms."

Andy seems to be putting into words an experience of God that many of us in church take for granted. When we come to worship, God comes and meets with us. This fact is truly staggering. But we need to remember that Andy is also talking about his first encounter with God. His words are a testimony of the way that God by his Spirit became real for him in that evening meeting. They show how worship and conversion do have a place together. But there is something else about Andy's words which I find quite remarkable.

This description is deeply theological and extremely biblical, yet it has not come from any kind of correct or approved church teaching or even from a long period of personal study. Andy has simply thought about what God has done in his life. He is not repeating the well worn phrases about conversion which we hear so often in a church context. He has had to find his own way of speaking about God. Many new converts speak with refreshing honesty, just like Andy, but over time they learn the jargon which we use in our churches and they lose their more natural and often more descriptive ways of speaking about God.

If alternative worship is to bring something new into the life of the Church then surely it will be these much more dynamic and personally relevant ways of talking about God. Instead of allowing Christian jargon to take over, we need to encourage people like Andy to stick with their way of speaking about what God is doing in their lives. When we come to planning services and getting people up front to preach, we should try to ensure that they use their own creative ways of speaking because this will set the tone for the whole of our worship. When young people speak about God in their own cultural phrases based on their own experience in the context of Christian worship, something new starts to happen. Most language used in church is quite formal, in fact most of the accents we hear in Church come from the educated and the upper class groups of society.

If alternative worship is to be truly "alternative" then it needs to allow for different voices and accents. If youth culture is characterized by informal expressions and ways of speaking, then so should worship which is based on that culture.

Open to God

Tom's experience was somewhat different:

"The worship time allowed me to think through what I learned about God during the week. I didn't feel restricted, I could let what I was feeling flood out. It was my first experience of being with God, allowing him into me for the

first time. I let myself open up and really think about God
and let him come to me. It was a blind thing, I just let him
in, I experienced him. Letting God become part of you. It's
not something that you can do cold. The worship time on
the holiday was a plateau, it brought together everything
that had happened during the week. Worship sparked off
a need to know more, what I'd got that evening I was really
scared of losing, I wanted it to continue and not fade away.''

Tom had heard the Gospel message on the holiday, but he
still needed some space to work things out. Interestingly
enough Tom talks about the experience at both an intellectual
and at an experimental level. He tried to work things out, but
he also needed to open himself up. To create a time for
reflection, silence and prayer is not to deny the more
intellectual side of turning to Christ. In fact the individual
young people can respond to the space provided in a time of
worship in the way that best suits them. But the crucial thing
here is that Tom needed an environment in which to reflect
and then make his decision to risk himself with God. As Tom
says he was working blind, but God met him in the silence
and in the words of Scripture.

It is a vital aspect of mission amongst young people that they
need help in opening themselves up to God. The crowded
room, the candles, the silence and the words of encouragement
from the Bible provided an atmosphere that made prayer much
easier for both Andy and Tom. They were able to quieten their
minds and reflect on the Gospel message in a peaceful haven
where God could touch them in a life-changing way.

People power

Tom said that you can't open up to God cold, and of course
he's hit the nail on the head. But what is it that warms us up
for God? Wilson told me that for him it was mainly the people
who were around him in the worship.

''I was brought up with God and taught to believe in him,
I thought I knew God, but I really only knew about him.
I was really moved by the atmosphere at the worship, it was
like 'total peace', everyone loved each other. I sensed God
was there through everyone, it was their attitudes, niceness,
harmony, mutual respect for everyone. At the worship we
were all in the same predicament, we wanted to know more
about God. It gave you a common bond. With people it feels
good, feels more open, feels closer, it's like a linking of souls
through the Holy Spirit.''

Going away with a group of young people is nearly always
a special event. For a short while you can experience a
communal feeling which is rare in everyday life. Of course it
is possible to misuse this very powerful experience and try to
control young people through group pressure. But having said
this it is hard to ignore what Wilson has to say, since during
the two years following that event he has been totally free to
go his own way and reject the experience if he wanted to. If
we take what Wilson says at face value then a very exciting
prospect emerges.

The people Wilson refers to were nearly all non-Christians
who were experiencing worship for the first time. They were
reaching out to God together as a group, and this fact is
extremely important. Most young people have strong peer
relationships. Youth culture is to a large extent a patchwork
of different individuals who identify strongly with each other
and create groups. They dress alike, they listen to the same
kinds of music, they share common hopes and in some cases
they share a common name, such as metallers or punks.
Alternative worship will be, to a large extent, shaped by these
kinds of friendship networks and approaches to common
style.

But young people also bond together in groups as a kind of
survival mechanism. It is their way of sorting out their common
problems. When Wilson talks about the worship time as being

special he is highlighting the need to take very seriously the role of teenage friendship groups in worship. It could perhaps be said that when the young people on the holiday decided to worship, they were in fact supporting each other in the journey of faith.

This aspect of youth culture is extremely important if we want to see alternative worship develop in our local area. We must look not just for the conversion of individuals but for the transformation of groups of teenagers in the light of the Gospel. From these friendship groups a distinctive Christian culture can emerge. The development of new forms of Christian worship will be very much a group activity. The young people will support each other as they seek to stay within their culture and local community while working out what being a Christian means for them. The group feel of alternative worship is a key element which youth culture brings to a renewed Church.

Worship points the way forward

This chapter has highlighted the need for worship to be a regular part of our plan for outreach to young people. This is important not simply because it works and young people become Christians. There is also the crucial factor that it is out of these refreshingly new experiences of God that alternative worship grows.

When someone asks me how to do alternative worship, my first response is normally to recommend that they ask the young people they know. We need to stop thinking of ourselves as experts who provide the right kind of spiritual insight to help young people. We become the learners. Young people react to a Bible passage or a piece of religious music or whatever it is and tell us what it means for them in their lives. In listening to Wilson, Andy and Tom I was finding out how God was leading them. I was not telling them what they should do. My role was simply to read the passage from Isaiah and allow them to be touched by the Word of God as the Spirit began to move.

But there is more to this process than simply providing material for young people to experience in worship. How can we help them grow in their distinctive kind of faith? That is the topic for the next chapter.

3 · Learning in a Vacuum

Everyone has to learn how to worship. I found my first visit to church bewildering. There were so many things I didn't understand. For young people starting to express their faith within their own culture, learning to worship on a regular basis is extremely demanding. If they are to grow a distinctive and vibrant new expression of Christian worship, we need to pay attention to this "learning factor".

Within a church setting this problem is fairly straightforward because there are already established patterns for Christian worship. But alternative worship is not about following along already existing paths. It is a kind of exploration, a journey into the unknown.

So how do we help young people on this journey? A good place to start is to look at how we ourselves learn to worship.

He lives within my heart

The experience of meeting Christ for the first time is often profound. It is like a fountain out of which worship flows. With Andy, Wilson and Tom we saw how they quite naturally responded to God's touch on their lives, and new and exciting expressions of Christian worship can result from such experiences. It is tempting therefore to assume that alternative worship could just evolve naturally from this starting point when God begins to affect the lives of young people. But this is a little too simple.

People don't learn to worship in a vacuum. We learn how to worship from one another – just as each of us learned how to pray.

Prayer for me did not come naturally. I had to learn from other people what I was meant to do, first by going along to prayer meetings and listening to other people pray, then reading the odd book about prayer. But things only really took off when I started to experiment myself with different forms of prayer.

We need other people's expressions of faith to use as a starting point for our own. I remember sitting in a prayer meeting hearing people pray out loud for the first time. It seemed very strange, but eventually I was ready to launch myself onto the open prayer scene and was about to produce my first fully made up prayer out loud! I was very nervous but in the end I was able to put a few thoughts together because I had learned how to do it from other more experienced people. I used the same sorts of phrases as the people around me, and it was only comparatively recently that I felt able to be more myself in these prayer times. Of course the need to let others understand and join in with my prayer dictates that I must follow the "rules" of praying out loud to some extent. I can't chant meaningless phrases or stand on one leg and hum, even if that is what I normally do in my quiet times! What is true for learning to pray is also true for other aspects of the Christian life.

Church culture

The rules that operate in an open prayer meeting are just the tip of the iceberg. Learning to worship in the Christian church involves each of us in a complicated cultural system. It includes the way we speak, think and look at life, not just how we act in church or at a prayer meeting. Growing as a Christian means slowly coming to terms with this cultural system and learning how to work within it.

Talking about the Christian faith as a cultural system is not to deny that God inspires us and guides us as we learn to be Christians. God is involved in all the processes by which we learn to pray. The fact that I needed to learn how to pray by listening to other people just shows how much God takes into account our humanity. Christian worship is divinely inspired but it is also the work of human beings.

Working the system

The culture of the local church seems so inflexible and timeless that our task of helping young people to grow in their faith is far from easy. Peter Berger in his book *The Social Reality of Religion* talks about culture under three headings: objectivation, internalization and externalization.[1] These headings suggest to me a three-stage approach to meeting this need.

1. *Objectivation:* Each one of us is born into a culture. We have to learn how to read, how to write, what to do and not to do at the meal table. Culture exists all around us as an external reality. If we want to play, then we have to learn the rules.

2. *Internalization:* Culture does not just exist outside us. We carry it around in our heads. I know that I am English. I was born in England, I speak English. All of this could have been different, but the fact that I was born and brought up in England has given me particular perspectives on life. These perspectives are open to change and revision but they are nevertheless part of me. Each one of us has taken our culture into our selves. We have internalized ways of looking not just at ourselves but also at everyone else in the world.

3. *Externalization:* People create culture. Human beings are creative and culture is the accumulation of all our creativity. Language is a good example of this. When we first start to speak we are told what everything is called, but have you ever thought about where these names come from? Someone must have been the first person to use the word "sky" when looking

up. Someone decided to call the moon "the moon". In the book of Genesis we are told that God brought all the animals to Adam and Adam gave them names. But we all participate in the creative shaping of our language, inventing more words and finding new ways to use old words. Young people are very much involved in the evolution of culture because much of what they create is new. They make their mark on fashion, music, graphic design, codes of behaviour, and many other areas of our culture.

Learning to worship

Objectivation, internalization and externalization can be applied to the way young people learn to worship. Young Christians need to go through various different stages as they move towards alternative worship in church. We need to plan discipleship bearing this process in mind.

In Oxford we have tried to work on this issue by devising a discipleship process which helps young people to move on by having two different sorts of meetings. The first meeting called Worship is a regular weekly get-together where young people can experience the different aspects of Christian worship in a very informal and unstructured setting.[2] We all cram together in a large sitting room, much like the holiday meeting I described. The second meeting is our alternative worship service: JOY. These two different meetings give a simple progression to our discipleship which allows room for young people to learn in their own way.

For successful alternative worship the final creative stage, what Peter Berger calls externalization, is crucial. But we can't start at this point. Young people need to be given enough time and space to progress through the learning stages at a pace they find comfortable.

If young people are to learn to worship they also need to become acquainted with traditional patterns of church culture. The danger is that they will get stuck at this first stage, modelling themselves on what already exists. Of course we should not blame them for this, but as their guides we need to be imaginative enough to help them develop into the third and much more creative stage of their development. Getting this right, I admit, is very difficult.

1. *Coming to terms with worship*

When young people first come to the Worship they are faced with a totally new way of being together as a group. In the normal run of things they wouldn't sing together, or listen to a talk or spend a few minutes in silence praying. These aspects of Christian worship need a little getting used to. The Worship session we run introduces them to some of these approaches to worship in a way which is non-threatening and easy to understand. There's little chance of feeling left out or on the edge of things because everyone is roughly at the same place. We try to maintain a relaxed atmosphere where young people can be themselves, so it is okay, for instance, for them to smoke or swear or even to burst out laughing at awkward moments.

For the newcomer this setting for worship is very useful because it does not demand very much commitment. Yet over a period this simple meeting allows us to introduce parts of the Christian tradition in easy-to-assimilate bite-sized chunks. One reason why young people find the experience of going to church so threatening is because it is like being thrown into the deep end of a swimming pool when you are just learning to swim!

In our worship session we try to share the skills of Christian worship as well as ideas about God. If we are going to sing a song then from time to time we will talk about how to worship by singing. We explain that we can use the words of the song to speak to God. When we pray we start with very simple exercises in prayer. We might suggest a few simple words to say to God or maybe we ask them to tell God about what has happened to them that day. When we read the Bible we use fairly short passages and invariably leave a good deal of time for discussion in small groups about what the passage means.

This approach enables the young people to be introduced very gently to the Christian tradition without being overwhelmed by the culture of the Church. Issues are presented in readily digestible ways. The young people are more likely to be able to stay in touch with their own culture because they can slowly adapt what they are learning about the Christian faith to their own cultural framework.

2. *Let's get spiritual*

New Christians are faced with enormous changes in the way they look at the world. As we grow in the Christian life, the Spirit of Jesus transforms every aspect of our lives. We start to see everything differently. In helping young people to grow in the faith we need to make room for this restructuring of their internal world. But because their cultural frameworks are likely to be very different from our own, we often don't know what this transformation should look like for them. Issues which we see as important may not be on their horizons at all. On the other hand they may well be asking questions about which we are totally clueless! One consolation is that God is not at all ignorant of the kinds of problems they face. The Spirit is working in these young people to raise questions and to challenge them about their lifestyles. We need to be sensitive to both the young people and the Spirit as we plan our discipleship.

In our worship session we make sure that a good deal of time is given over to discussion in small groups. The young people meet in friendship groups which reflect the culture of their particular area. This allows them to talk about being Christians in terms which make sense in their own local environment and culture. We encourage them to help each other and support each other in prayer. But we also give them time to reflect as a group on passages of the Bible. In this

way they can slowly start to internalize the Christian faith
at their own pace.

3. *Creating worship*

Helping young people to express their own ideas and
perspectives in worship is the life blood of alternative worship.
Much of what happens in our churches is far from creative.
On the whole we are expected to be passive consumers of
church services. Alternative worship strives to be different
precisely because it is based on involvement and creativity. But
people do need to learn how to be creative.

Learning to be creative in worship is a mysterious process,
and some people find it easier than others. We find that by
varying the kinds of activities we include in our worship,
more young people are able to express their faith for
themselves. For example, using art work and drawing in
worship has opened up creativity for a whole new bunch
of young people.

We try, as much as possible, to use songs and ideas that
young people themselves have written. The way people write
songs is a good example of how this more creative stage of
worship can be handled.

My job as a youth worker involves me in spending time
with young people who are in rock bands. I am able to be
part of their learning process right from the first time they
pick up a guitar until they make their first recording. One
thing that has impressed me is that no one – apart from God,
of course – creates from nothing. Young people learning to
play the guitar start by copying other people's styles. At first
they are all fingers and thumbs, but soon they become
proficient at playing this material. Then they realize that if
they want to get anywhere they must start to write their own
songs.

Most people start with an idea from someone else's work
which they twist a bit to make it sound different. It might be
a basic drum beat, a phrase in the lyrics or even the way that

one chord follows another chord. This might sound all wrong to the outsider, but even the greatest of musicians work this way. Take Paul Simon's use of African rhythms on his Gracelands album, for instance. Here we have a Western musician openly using other people's music as a starting point for his own creativity. He has been much criticized for this, and yet what he has done openly the rest of us do without mentioning it. We do this because we all create using the raw materials of other people's creations.

This process is exactly what happens when young people begin to move into the more creative stage of learning to worship. In creating worship themselves they have to start with the raw material which the Church has already created. This raw material will be the external reality of the Church's tradition – the accumulation of songs, ways of praying, creeds, hymns and rituals which Christian people down the centuries have created. In most church settings we either repeat what is handed down to us, or we rely on experts to provide us with new forms of worship which we can copy. In encouraging alternative forms of worship we need to avoid taking the easy option of repeating established patterns of worship.

This is not to say we must reject ancient and beautiful forms of worship. Instead we need to see them as a resource which needs to be "twisted" a little bit, or combined with something with which it has previously not been joined. In this way we can help young people to create their own worship using tradition as the building blocks.

As an example of this, in JOY we use the regular Anglican liturgy for the Communion service, but the priest says the old form of the words over a dance track which is played over the P.A. system. This simple idea has transformed the liturgy. In fact the priest quite often uses the beat of the music as he speaks the words and the result is a new and exciting creation: youth culture and ritual combined in a sort of rap! How this sort of combination can come about is the subject of the next two chapters.

NOTES

1. See *The Social Reality of Religion* by Peter Berger, p14.
2. The Worship meeting is described in much more detail in *Youth Culture and the Gospel*, pp158–62.

4 · Mixing It with Youth Culture

Alternative worship involves a new relationship between the tradition of the Church and youth culture. The last chapter concentrated on the need for young people to learn the vocabulary of worship before they can be set free to create for themselves. This learning process, however, is only one part of the puzzle. What young people bring with them from their culture needs to end up as part of the mix.

If church tradition is to interact with youth culture to form alternative worship, it involves much more than simply including modern music in a church service. The ingredients which youth culture bring to the mix can be very distinctive. This chapter explores a few of these ingredients and shows what impact they are likely to have on the creation of alternative worship.

Creating your own identity

Young people create their own cultures and sub-cultures by the choices they make when they go shopping. They are creative consumers: they make their choices of consumer items in a symbolic way.

This symbolic role for items of clothing or different styles of bikes or skate boards is so common we hardly notice it. We all know of people like the young lad who hears about a band from one of his older brothers. He buys their record and becomes aware that the members of the band dress a certain way. A few weeks later he adopts their pattern of dress, and in doing so moves closer to all the other young people in his neighbourhood or around the country who also dress that way.

Such choices are not simply about individual taste, they are about the way young people create their identities.

Teenagers often feel very strongly about the clothes that they wear. This is not really surprising when you realize that their choice of clothes is closely linked with identity. Identity is the most important issue that young people are dealing with. Questions of identity surround the adolescent, including sexuality, occupation, and educational opportunities. Forming groups by adopting a particular way of dressing does not resolve these issues, but it is one way of building a safe, understood environment to which they can retreat from time to time and from which they can launch themselves at life.

The fact that young people create identity for themselves in this way is extremely significant for the development of alternative worship. We need to be fully aware of the reasons why young people are so deeply attached to the various styles of youth culture. We also need to appreciate that young people actively take part in the construction of their own identity.

Alternative worship which is based on youth culture will need to be open enough to allow young people to be able to construct their own Christian identities. Most church contexts do not offer this kind of freedom. In general we are told by someone else what God expects of us. This is especially true when we first become Christians. After the initial choice to follow Christ the rest of the package, it seems, is really not up for grabs. Our identity as a Christian is like a ready-made suit of clothes and we can either wear it or not wear it.

For alternative worship young people need to sort out how God is challenging them to live the Christian life. This does not mean they can do whatever they like and call it a Christian approach to life. It simply means actively seeking out what God expects of them.

Symbolically speaking

Youth cultures are constructed from a whole series of choices about style. By style here I don't just mean different kinds of clothes. It is, for instance, a matter of style to hang around inside a shopping precinct. Some white working-class young people in Britain have adopted words and phrases which were first used by urban black people in the USA. This too is style. Aspects of group behaviour and language as well as choices in fashion go to make up young people's style. But what so often gives this style impact is the way it has been constructed.

Young people's style is created by the way different and often contrasting elements are taken and used in combination with each other. The other day I saw a young girl walking down the road wearing a very colourful cotton summer dress. She was also wearing a large bulbous pair of Dr Marten's boots. This kind of juxtaposition of different types of clothing can't just be dismissed as fashion. These two different items have a significance, they are symbolic. The flowery cotton summer dress has always been associated with a particular kind of femininity. The Dr Marten boot is more often seen on a working man's foot, or perhaps a skinhead's. When the Bovver boot meets the Laura Ashley dress a dialogue at a symbolic level is taking place! The masculine and possibly threatening message of the Bovver boot clashes with the innocent summery sexuality of the dress. At a time when the traditional roles for men and women are being redefined, a girl who adopts this kind of style is sending out a message about where she stands.

Alternative worship needs to operate in the same symbolic way. In our worship in JOY we have used tough news photographs of people suffering while we celebrate the Communion. The two images jar with each other, yet they also complement each other. Rave-type dancing in church is another combination from which so many creative connections can be made. In the first place there's the question of people's sexuality. The Christian Church has never really been very positive about sexuality. Yet today's young people are in the forefront of the emphasis on health and physical fitness. Unlike the Church they generally have a positive view of their bodies and a healthy sense of sexuality. Rave-type dancing in church is therefore a statement about an alternative, and equally valid, Christian approach to our bodies and to sexuality in general.

This sort of dancing in church is also important because it introduces a chaotic and informal element into worship.

Informal worship

Most young people find the formal nature of church very difficult to handle. We all sit in rows facing the front and the service is generally fairly well scripted. There are strict codes of behaviour – you can't eat a packet of crisps in church! In some churches there is even an unwritten rule that you have to wear your best clothes.

When young people get together they generally organize themselves in much less formal ways. At a party or a rave people are free to dance when they like and how they like. It's okay if you want to chat to a friend or go out for a bit of fresh air. When young people meet up with each other they normally sit in small groups. Some prefer to lean on each other or sit on each other's laps. If they discuss something they often all talk at once.

Organizing a church service which reflects a measure of this kind of informality can be quite tricky. But periods of dance can break up the more rigid structures which we normally associate with church. It is also possible to organize the seating so that people can choose how they sit. In JOY everyone sits on the floor so they can arrange things how they want. A service can be varied by allowing time for people to discuss issues in small groups, so that the whole event is not led from the front.

Informal styles of leadership

Young people need leaders. Many of them want to receive help and guidance on all sorts of areas. The popularity of the problem page in teenage magazines is just one indication of this. But it is equally true that young people by and large reject leadership which is officially sanctioned or appointed.

I'm always interested in the way boys at the school where I help out react to the teachers. Some teachers are respected, others are not. What makes a teacher "all right" is usually the fact that they have made some effort to relate well to the boys. They exercise their authority with a sensitivity and humour which earns them respect. While these teachers may well be quite strict, they are not usually resented for it. The boys respond well even to discipline because of the kind of person the teacher is. In short, a teacher has to earn respect from the boys. Teachers command authority because the young people give it to them.

This sort of dynamic is of course common throughout life. Some managers are seen as good by the workers and others are not. Some vicars are respected and some are not. But for young people this informal response to those who wish to guide and lead them is of paramount importance. If we want to see alternative worship grow in our local church then we need to take full account of the kinds of leadership styles that young people respond to. We can't simply rely on a system which appoints leaders from above. People are leaders because others listen to what they have to say. To operate this sort of leadership in a mainstream church is difficult because it doesn't fit the authoritarian structures of most churches. But alternative worship must be alternative in the way it appoints leaders and in the way those leaders exercise their role.

Working within informal networks

Youth culture has been described as "proto communities"[1]. This refers to the sense of togetherness formed around informal and transitory popular symbols and events which have a power to create values and attitudes. The reaction to the disaster at Hillsborough football stadium amongst Liverpool supporters is a fine example of the power of a group's leisure activities. The sight of the Anfield pitch covered in scarves and flowers in tribute to those who died was unforgettable. It was not only a football club that was in mourning but a whole city and nation.

In the subsequent services of remembrance in the Roman Catholic and then in the Anglican cathedrals in Liverpool there was a sense of two worlds meeting. On the one hand there was the informal popular symbols of the football teams' colours, on the other hand there was the "official" religious symbolism – a cathedral. In a sense the teams' colours clashed culturally with a church service, seeming out of place as symbols from popular working-class culture, whereas the cathedral is a bastion of English middle-class values. But there was also a sense in which these services showed the Church starting to identify with ordinary people in a way which was very apt and natural. This feeling I'm sure was due in no small measure to the work of the two bishops in Liverpool. But there was perhaps an even more important reason why these services seemed to "fit" in an official church setting.

Looking at the colours of Liverpool and Everton on display among the congregation it became clear that supporting a football club was not simply an insignificant Saturday afternoon activity. Here a group of people faced tragedy together. Supporting a football team involved people in a community which could affect them quite profoundly. In their sense of identification with each other they were living out some of the things that we in the Church often just talk about. Surely here in the world of "popular culture" we could see what Paul meant when he said that in the body of Christ, "If one part of the body suffers, all the other parts suffer with it" (1 Corinthians 12:26).

Live Aid is another example of the power of popular culture to effect a change in attitudes and values amongst the whole nation. A significant aspect of the concert at Wembley and in the United States was that a community of people had worked to get this amazing event off the ground. A friend of mine chatted to someone in a pub a few weeks before the event. This chance conversation resulted in my friend getting involved in the production of the Live Aid programme. He, along with hundreds of other people, gave an enormous amount of time and energy to the event. Sometimes he worked for two whole days without sleeping to get all the art work for the programme in on time. But those working on the production of Live Aid were not the only ones who felt involved. Those of us sitting at home watching on TV were just as moved by the whole event. Suddenly the issue of starvation in Africa was on all our agendas, we all gained a conscience and many of us gave money to the appeal. For a brief while a "proto community" came into being.

What is amazing about these sorts of proto communities is that we can actually belong to a great many of them. We move easily from one informal grouping to another and all the time we are participating in a way of looking at the world. This world view is not passed down to us by other people, we are actually a part of its construction. Live Aid was significant because so many of us took it seriously. Other such events which have tried to copy Live Aid have been less successful. The reason is simple: fewer people took them up as being important.

But proto communities do not have to be massive events involving large numbers of people. It is quite possible for small groups of people to generate a common culture which has its own effect on their lives. A local American Football team may not have a great many people turning up at its games, but it will create its own language, values, and attitudes. This micro-culture is sure to have an extraordinarily powerful impact on the lives of the people involved with the team.

Alternative worship which seeks to be based on youth culture needs to come to terms with the characteristics of proto communities. In the first place we need to be in touch with the concerns that young people bring with them to worship.

The sight of Liverpool and Everton scarves in the cathedral services after Hillsborough was unusual. In alternative worship this sort of association needs to be a regular part of the construction of the service. The signs and symbols of young people's lives need to find a place in the normal repertoire of our worship. This is not just a gimmick. It is a sign that Jesus is Lord of all. It shows that every aspect of our lives can be brought to God in worship. His concerns are our concerns. In this way we deny anything is secular, for nothing is outside the scope of Christian worship.

But proto communities present another and much more difficult challenge for Alternative worship. Church membership tends to be fairly static and permanent. Proto communities, on the other hand, are fluid and temporary. To what extent should an alternative worship service reflect this aspect of youth culture? Should we be surprised if young people associate with our worship in much the same way as they do with proto communities?

Our experience both in Oxford Youth Works and in JOY has been that young people do tend to drift in and out of relationship with us. So how can we maintain a service when the congregation's loyalty seems to ebb and flow somewhat? I believe we need to be willing to allow young people a good deal of freedom in how much commitment they give to a worship service. At the same time, however, we should help them develop a more mature and stable worshipping life. This, as with most things, involves sensitivity and also a willingness to keep things in balance. If we push young people too hard we will lose them, but if we fail to challenge them we shall ultimately be letting them down.

All change

Youth culture is extremely creative and it is always changing. In fact for many of us the pace of change is quite bewildering. New types of music hit the charts all the time. One day an item of clothing is "in", the next day it's "out". Much of this is fuelled by the industries which feed off the tastes of young consumers. But young people themselves are also creatively interacting with the media and the fashion industry.

Changing styles are partly a response to wider social and economic issues. It is interesting to look at the quite remarkable changes in teenage style during the 1980s and early 1990s in the light of high unemployment followed by economic boom and then the emergence of global and environmental issues[2]. In the 1980s we saw some unemployed young people adopting punk style and sniffing glue on our streets, while others dressed all in black and called themselves Goths. In the 1990s rave culture has restored aspects of the 'sixties psychedelic era with the addition of baseball caps and baggy jeans. These styles show a reaction at a symbolic level to the changes in society. Young people from different social groups experience the changes in our economic and political life as much as anyone and their style is a reflection of this fact.

Youth culture is in part an escape from the world, a kind of substitute for involvement in the wider society, but is also a dialogue with that society. Teenage style creates safe group identities to which young people can feel they belong. But the kind of behaviour and style which is adopted within these groups is very often a reaction to issues such as unemployment, homelessness and education. Alternative worship will inevitably not only reflect these concerns but also have to become part of the dialogue with the wider society. If our worship is using the symbols and style of youth culture, then the church will become involved with some of the issues which they are a reaction to. It is hard to estimate how significant this aspect of alternative worship will be. Suffice it to say that it will be a contrast to the insulated world which currently exists in many of our churches. In many ways the average church feels like a peaceful back water cut off from the mainstream of everyday life, with its own inward-looking culture. By incorporating the symbols of youth culture into our worship we will suddenly find ourselves part of the flow of popular ideas and concerns. Our worship will be much more sharply focused on the kinds of problems that affect young people, and we will start to address how Jesus makes sense of issues such as unemployment, racial prejudice, violence and poverty. We will not be able to avoid it because the young people themselves will bring these issues into church with them.

NOTES

1. For more on this see Paul Willis, *Common Culture*, pp141–45.
2. This aspect of teenage style is considered in more depth in *Youth Culture and the Gospel*, chapter 5.

5 · Imagination: Putting Worship Together

Worship is deeply related to imagination. The great leader of the reformation, Martin Luther, speaking of his Christian experience said, "I close my eyes and I have a picture of a man on a cross in my heart"[1]. This sort of "imaginative" approach to God forms a part of each person's prayer life. Of course we may not think in pictures like Luther, but we do form an impression of what God is like and to do this we must use our imagination.

For alternative worship we must learn how to picture a new kind of worship. And this needs imagination. It is imagination which helps us to see how to bring together the two basic elements in alternative worship: youth culture and the Christian tradition.

Letting the imagination run free

Imagination can be a scarce commodity in adult life. As we grow up we often stop functioning at an imaginative level. If we need to rely upon our imagination to create alternative worship then we shall have to re-learn how to use it. The best way to do this is to revisit childhood and rediscover how children use their imaginations.

Story-telling and imaginative play form an important part of most children's lives. But play is not just idle leisure time activity. Children can use play as a way to sort out the big issues in their lives. It can tell us a tremendous amount about what's on their mind. For instance children who have been sexually or physically abused are often encouraged to act out their experiences in their play. This kind of play is not simply a clever way for the police to get their evidence. The children actually use their play times to wrestle with what has happened to them and start to deal with their pain. This sort of play has been explored in a specifically religious context by Jerome Berryman.

In his book *Godly Play* Jerome Berryman describes how imagination and play form the basis for religious education in the Sunday school class he runs each week. He has designed his classroom to allow the children to have free access to a number of different learning resources and toys, each relating to a specific Bible story or characters. These are kept in a variety of shelves, cupboards and boxes, but each of them should be seen as a crucial story or symbol which together form the Christian faith. For instance, one shelf in his classroom holds statues representing the Holy Family (Joseph, Mary and the baby Jesus). On the right of the Holy Family stands the Good Shepherd, and to the right again there is the Light. Of course Jesus spoke of himself as both Good Shepherd and as Light, and so these are there right in the centre of the classroom display. But these statues are not simply decoration, they are there to be played with.

Each Sunday school lesson involves the telling of a Bible story. As the teacher recounts the story he or she will "show" the story by using the materials from the shelves as illustrative material. After the story has been told the children are invited to respond to what they have heard, or to another story from a previous lesson, in any way they want to. This is not a free for all, in fact there are a large number of artistic materials, including paints, modelling clay and paper available for the children to use to work through the stories that they have heard.

What is amazing is that the children seem to use the space when they are painting or drawing to sort out how the biblical stories and symbols make sense of what is going on in their lives. One child may be worried about death, another by a problem of pain. In their art they use the images from the Bible to work on what is troubling them, but remarkably they will often mix and match the biblical characters and stories. This may at first appear to be random, but Jerome points out that often the different biblical characters and stories are associated for very good symbolic reasons. In fact he encourages this kind of "playful" association precisely because it provides a place for the children to resolve faith issues in the context of the Sunday school.

See how the children play

There is a sense in which all kinds of alternative worship are like Jerome Berryman's Sunday school class. Any new approach to worship will involve the imaginative use of religious symbols. This could simply be the association of two things which don't ordinarily seem to go together, e.g. rock music and the communion service. Or it could be the use of a familiar symbol in a new way, e.g. popular styles of rave dancing in worship. But however the symbols are arranged or manipulated, it is important to see that there is a reason. It is at this point that I think the idea of the playful use of imagination can help us to understand what exactly we are doing in worship.

In *Godly Play* Jerome Berryman describes how the children use religious symbols to work out how faith works. For instance a child may paint an extremely violent picture, but when you examine it closely in one corner there is a character who remains unaffected by the turbulence. The child explains that this is the Good Shepherd. Jerome interprets this as the child's attempt to deal with problems associated with death and violence. The picture is a symbolic approach to the issue. The world is full of trouble, but Jesus, the Good Shepherd, remains strong and able to help whatever.

Some children apparently work with the same sorts of images week after week. Their pictures repeat common themes, but then suddenly change. This happens, he says, when the particular faith issue which has been troubling the child has, for the time being, been resolved. When the time is right the child will move on to other faith issues and the symbols will change, but all the time they will be exploring and experimenting with their understanding of faith.

Worship and play

When we sit down to plan worship, part of the process involves an element of symbolic play. Just like the child in the Sunday school, we use religious ideas and symbols as a way to make sense of life. One way to look at this process is to see each of the various elements of a service – the music, the art work, the architecture of the worship space, the words people say – as pieces of a symbolic jigsaw puzzle. The difference is that this puzzle has an infinite variety of ways to fit together and as you vary the shape of the puzzle different pictures begin to emerge. One example of this is to vary the seating.

The way we arrange the seating in worship is significant. If everyone sits in a circle then you have a feeling of being equal and together in worship. If one person sits on a raised platform with everyone else facing them the message is more authoritarian. In alternative worship we need to experiment with the seating. By moving things around and trying out different combinations we can eventually discover what works for our service. This playing with the seating is essentially based on imagination and experimentation. We see the possibilities of arranging the room one way and then we try it out to see what happens.

Playing at worship

Imaginative play in worship is not simply the pursuit of change for change's sake. It is essential if we are going to start to deal with young people's faith issues. Just like the child, we need to feel that life makes sense. In alternative worship young people wrestle with their problems by addressing them symbolically.

For most of us a major issue of faith is suffering. Life is painful, friends we know and love die, parents split up, we see famine and war on the daily news. Yet most church services seem to concentrate on presenting a reassuring and loving environment and a God who is all-powerful and loves us. The implication is that by going to worship and entering this safe world we can be strengthened to face life again. We need to be comforted, but in the face of real suffering this kind of worship does wear a bit thin. The problem in singing songs like "Jesus' love is very wonderful" is that they can ring a bit hollow if we don't ever acknowledge the problems which we all face from time to time. Making sense of these apparent contradictions and then setting out to live a healthy and fulfilling life is one of the most difficult challenges we face as Christians. One of the best ways worship can encourage us in this direction is by helping us face suffering head on.

In one of our services at JOY we decided that we wanted to look at the question of family relationships. The rest of this chapter describes how we used the various parts of the service in our symbolic play.

A service outline

1. We used the reading from the Old Testament about "Honouring our parents".

2. A number of people told the stories of their family lives. One of these involved a hard-hitting and heartrending story of abuse within a family.

3. Throughout the service the central screen displayed a massive psychedelic cross.

4. After one of the stories we read aloud a short meditation about holding on to a coin in your hand so tightly that no

one could get at it. The coin was like some hurt or pain in our lives which we didn't want anyone to get close to. Prayer was then seen as the process which encouraged us slowly to let go of the coin. We then left some space for people to experience this approach to prayer for themselves.

5. One of the songs we sang was written by a young person who had experienced pain in the family and it relates this experience to the death of Christ on the cross. Here are the lyrics.

> You died on a wooden cross, with thorns on your head
> Nails through your hands and feet, and a sword through your side
> You tell me you understand the thorns in my words
> The nails that still pierce my heart
> And the sword through my soul.
> Is this believing?
> Or am I dreaming?

6. As we sang the song, the screens displayed pictures illustrating human suffering. One was ''The Scream'' by Munch which shows a cartoon-like figure with mouth open in the action of screaming. Another was a detail of Picasso's ''Geurnica'', portraying a woman looking up at the sky yelling her grief at the death of her child whom she holds in her hands. We also showed a particularly powerful and graphic picture of Christ's agony on the cross.

This service involved a variety of different approaches to the same topic. We were able to ''play'' with these different elements creating new combinations which shed light on suffering and the death of Christ on the cross. In symbolic terms we were able to show that Jesus identifies with our suffering. He is by no means a stranger to pain. His death means that we can see him as a friend who has also ''gone through it'' and can embrace us in our suffering. But he does so whilst still bearing the marks of the nails in his own hands.

One woman came up to me after the service and said how much she had appreciated the fact that we were dealing with suffering honestly. She had spent the whole of the week nursing a dying child and she was left to comfort the child's parents when he eventually died. The service spoke powerfully to her precisely because it was an attempt to make sense of pain in the light of the Christian Gospel.

We desperately need this kind of symbolic play in the church if we are to create alternative worship. Imaginative experimentation will bring together the rich heritage of the Christian tradition with the issues and concerns of young people. Creativity has to have this kind of playful attitude if it is to be successful in enhancing alternative worship.

Using the word play may seem to belittle the profound nature of what was actually going on. That is by no means my intention. In fact the symbolic play of worship is a serious activity, and one that we should practise more and more in church. It links closely with the way youth culture plays with symbols in a search for meaning and identity.

NOTE

1. Quoted in John Dillenberger, *A Theory of Artistic Sensibilities*, p65.

6 · Everyday Ecstasy

I have often been challenged by the way St Francis of Assisi lived the Gospel, renouncing riches and caring for the poor. But I didn't realize how much of a Charismatic he was.

One day, apparently, St Francis sat down to have a meal with St Clare. "As the first dish was set before them, St Francis began to speak of God in so sweet, holy, lofty, and divine a way that St Francis himself, St Clare and her companion, and all who were at that modest little table, were caught up in mighty and abundant grace from the Most High that came upon them.

As they were thus sitting in ecstasy and lifting eyes and hands to heaven, the people of Assisi and Bettona and all along the road thought that the whole of St Mary of the Angels, the building, and the wood which surrounded it, were on fire, and an enormous conflagration enveloped the whole. So the men of Assisi ran hastily to save the building, firmly convinced it would burn down completely. When they arrived they found it unharmed and intact. Going in they found St Francis, St Clare and all their company in a divine ecstasy, all sitting at that most humble table clothed with virtue from on high."[1]

This simple tale about St Francis and St Clare is similar to the experience of God talked about in the more Charismatic parts of the Church today. In fact some people talk about a sense of God's presence as a daily event. I have to come clean here and say that I have also "experienced" God in an ecstatic way (although I have to admit it never stopped me eating dinner). As we have already seen, "experience" of God has often been at the root of young people starting and continuing in the Christian life.

Like when England beat France at rugby!

After one of our JOY services I talked to Stu, one of the local young people from Blackbird Leys Estate. Here's what he said about it.

> "I wanted to stand up and yell Yehhhhhhhhhhhh! God touched me, summut there made me happy. In the peace bit I felt like yellin out, 'I'm happy to be with you.' I felt like screaming out, 'I'm happy to be here.' Like when England beat France at rugby [the world cup was on at this time, a memorable day I have to agree!].
>
> Next morning I thought about the feeling I had and it just came back. In the bathroom I had a wash and I thought back for some reason to the night before to 'peace be with you', and for a split second it came back. God was with me at the church, God came again to let me know that he's there with me, not just in church, but also in the morning."

I was deeply moved when Stu told me this. God was reaching into his life in a new and life-changing way. But I also began to feel a little uneasy. While I was sure that God through the Holy Spirit was powerfully affecting Stu, I also believe very strongly that worship of God has to be more than some sort of emotional buzz. This was not born of scepticism about the Charismatic movement, and it certainly did not mean that I doubted what God was doing for Stu. My unease came from my experience of youth culture and the way our JOY service was starting to include elements from that culture in its worship.

Rave on

JOY, like many of the new alternative worship services in the Church at this time, is based around rave culture. For the uninitiated, raves are informal discotype dance parties. A rave can happen at an established club, but in our area, certainly during the summer time, they have been informal outdoor

events. The usual pattern is that a large group of young people
converge on some unsuspecting farmer's field, set up their
sound equipment and party until the early hours of the
morning. Needless to say this whole thing is illegal and large
police operations are mounted to try to stop the parties
happening. The young people usually rally together and form
a small convoy which heads out to the chosen spot. If the police
have wind of this the group simply make for another peaceful
and less protected rural spot. Once they are up and running
the police have no power to close them down without resorting
to the courts, and by the time these comparatively lengthy legal
niceties have been observed the farmer is left, after a sleepless
night, with a ruined crop and a litter-filled field! From the
young people's point of view the inconvenience caused to
other people is not a problem. If it feels good, do it!

The music at these raves is always provided by up-beat high
energy dance tracks, sometimes performed live, but more often
recorded just like at a normal disco. Raves have always been
strongly linked with drugs, in particular Ecstasy or "E" as most
people call it. Ecstasy is a chemical substance whose effect is
to give amazing amounts of energy and induce a sense of well
being which lifts people out of themselves into another "realm
of experience". It is not uncommon for young people to talk
of a kind of "madness" where you feel like you love everyone
and everything. Ecstasy comes in many forms, but essentially
it is a good-time drug which today is almost synonymous with
parties.

Adopting elements of rave culture into Christian worship
therefore poses some serious problems. We may offer young
people a misleading approach to God. I want to affirm people
like Stu in their experience of God, and the Charismatic
movement has opened up for me a more emotional response
to God in worship. Yet there is a real danger that we could
simply be substituting the Spirit for a drug-induced experience.
Instead of taking Es at a Rave you dance in church and get
an even better high. This would reduce Christian worship to

an experience of God which, though more healthy than taking drugs, is essentially a reduction of the Christian faith which verges on idolatry.

Majesteeee

For those of us brought up in Charismatic evangelical churches, the problem is complicated by our own tendency to reduce Christian worship to an experience. When I go to a worship session at one of the local churches there are times when I feel some sympathy with the young people who are confused on this issue. Which one of us can honestly say that at one time or another we have not confused the experience of God's presence in worship with the face of worship itself? If I don't "feel" God's presence in a service then I start to wonder if it was worthwhile. The "if it feels like God then it is God" attitude of the Charismatic Church is not a long way from the "if it feels good do it" attitude of most young people. Both are simply a reflection of a much wider cultural bias in our society.

Our present emphasis on the experience of the presence of God is not a bad thing. "Feeling" the presence of God is at the root of my own spiritual life. The Russian Orthodox writer Anthony Bloom says, "If we cannot meet God within, in the very depth of ourselves, our chances of meeting him outside ourselves are very remote." This, it seems to me, puts a note of caution on any attempt to rubbish the experiential side of Christian worship, and yet some sort of balance is needed.

In starting alternative worship services this issue needs to be addressed right from the start. While it is right to encourage young people to express their faith in their own cultural forms, we need to be alive to the fact that with these forms come all sorts of other messages and meanings. Those involved in alternative worship need to have a clear framework of what Christian worship is, and is not, meant to be.

Constructing this framework will need to be a group activity

involving young people, church authorities and other well
informed people. And this framework will need to be
continually revised and up-dated in the light of experience and
your own reading of the Bible. For these reasons I am very
reluctant to lay down hard and fast rules for anyone involved
in this work. However, looking at someone else's attempt at
sorting it all out can be helpful and so the rest of this chapter
gives some hints on my own answers to some of the questions.

We worship God

It might sound very obvious, but this is the place to start —
with worship of God. The Ten Commandments put it this way:
"I am the Lord your God, who rescued you from Egypt, where
you were slaves. Worship no God but me" (Deuteronomy
5:6–7). We probably feel that we live up to the demands of
this commandment, and of the second which forbids the
worship of idols. But it's not as straightforward as it seems.

It is easy to mistake the "experience of the presence of God"
for God himself. We need to continually remind ourselves that
God is not limited, contained or even to be predicted in our
feelings or emotions. Of course God does touch us very deeply,
but our feelings themselves are not "God". They may well
be the result of God's presence, but they should not be
confused with God himself.

This brings us to a further problem that we confront in
worship. Because our sense of the presence of God is often
the result of singing a few songs or taking communion, we
can start to see God's presence as an inevitable result of these
activities. In other words, if we sing the right kinds of songs
in the right kinds of ways with the right kinds of people then
we will be touched by God. This is a mistake because we do
not control God. We cannot dictate, predict or expect that God
will meet us in worship. To do so is to worship a non-God,
a God who no longer has free will, a God who is at our beck
and call. The true worship of God is something completely

different. It is a matter of faith and trust in a God who chooses to meet us and touch us with his life because that is his wish.

To meet this God is a transforming experience. In his presence we are turned upside down. In worship we enter into a new and disturbing world, a world where God is truly God. The effect of this revelation is that it destabilizes our comfortable human constructions. We are forced to revise our previous ideas about life as we gain a new perspective. As we worship we are aligning ourselves with this new perspective and becoming the means for its realization in life. To adopt this new perspective does not mean that we reject our previous culture but it does mean that we look for its transformation and redemption in the light of the revelation of God.[2]

Worship in Christ

If we want our worship to be Christian then it has to centre on Jesus. This again might seem very obvious, yet it is easy to lose sight of the fact that we see God truly revealed in the historical life of Christ as it is recorded in the gospels. In our worship we constantly need to be reflecting upon what Jesus said and what he did, for without this discipline we would very soon lose our way. It is also important to try to ensure that the whole of the life of Christ is represented in our worship. Many chorus books seem content to talk only about Jesus after the Ascension, as Lord or King or The Lamb. References to his daily life, the people he met and how he affected their lives, even the miracles, are often kept to a minimum. For worship to be ''in Christ'' it needs to affirm the earthly life of Jesus as the place where God became incarnate – where he took flesh, or in modern terms where the rubber meets the road. This ''earthed'' aspect of Christian worship needs to be taken very seriously.

God touches us not by taking us out of ourselves to another spiritual dimension, nor by addressing us in a loud manner from outside our world. Christian worship is based on the belief that God reveals himself within our culture. Jesus was both truly human and truly God, and Christian worship has a similar sort of a mix. On the one hand Christian worship is about an encounter with God who is wholly outside our experience, and yet this encounter always takes place within human culture.

Nowhere is this seen better than in the communion service for here we have bread and wine made with human hands, and yet God chooses to use them as the means to convey his grace to us. The bread and the wine are taken up by God and transformed into something holy. This is in no way to put down their material characteristics. God affirms the material, cultural world by using it as his place of self-revelation. Christian worship will always affirm the physical, everyday and ordinary parts of our lives as the place where God touches each of us.

So we cannot isolate the kind of intense experience Stu talks of and say that this alone is true worship. If we focus only on emotional highs, then we miss the fact that God wants to be a part of every aspect of our lives. Daily living in the presence of Christ is also worship. Work, rest and play are not just offered to us by the Mars Bar advertisement. The Spirit of God is with us inspiring us to be true to him in the way that we act and speak, all of the time.

Our concept of worship needs to be big enough to account for the daily presence of God in our lives. It will not always be dramatic or emotional. It is much more likely that these parts of our lives will simply begin to take on a new significance over a period of time. Nowhere is this aspect of worship more true than when we start to be involved in caring for the needy and the poor. Such caring is indeed worship, but it is rarely characterized by ecstatic experiences! Our understanding of worship needs to include every aspect of life — the mundane and the ecstatic. To worship truly we will need to live in obedience to God rather than chase religious experience.

Worship in the power of the Holy Spirit

Paul says that each of us, ''whether Jews or Gentiles, whether slaves or free, have been baptized into one body by the same Spirit'' (1 Corinthians 12:13). Worship in the Spirit is a corporate affair. It stems from the uniting and unifying presence of God's Spirit dwelling in each of us. This presents a serious challenge to young people, for in the long term any worship service based around youth culture will need to come to some sort of agreement with the wider Church. We belong to one another if we have been touched by Christ's Spirit, and our church life together needs to reflect this fact.

This does not mean that there must be uniformity in our worship or that we should set out to change young people into ordinary church-goers. It simply means that in the Spirit of God there is both unity and diversity. Paul's picture of the body of Christ (1 Corinthians 12:12–26) makes this point very clear. In the body of Christ we are united, but this does not affect our essential diversity. Both unity and diversity will be characteristics of all new types of worship. But the corporate nature of Christian worship means that we need each other in order that we may worship God.

The authentic activity of the Holy Spirit amongst us will inevitably result in Christian community. By Christian community I mean a group of people who are sharing their lives together and seeking to worship God together. For young people this aspect of Christian worship is both an affirmation of some parts of their culture and a challenge to others. On the one hand some young people form very tight groups which could be seen as a starting point for Christian community, but on the other hand young people can be very individualistic in their lifestyles and values. To be the body of Christ will involve young people in trusting relationships which may well be very new for them. They need each other in order that they may truly worship. This does not mean that we cannot experience God in our lives as individuals, but this experience always directs us towards corporate expressions of its life and energy.

This sense of community needs to be contrasted with the chemically induced sense of togetherness achieved by taking the drug Ecstasy. The problem with the rave scene is that you have to come home. It is a temporary madness which essentially involves a retreat into a "world of your own". Christian community is much more long term and it does not consist simply of sentiment, but grows from hard work over a long period of time. The work of the Spirit in our lives results in interdependence. However the Spirit leads us not only into unity, but also into a life of service in the world.

The Anglican communion service ends with these words: "Send us out in the power of your Spirit to live and work to your praise and glory." If what we do in church is to have any meaning at all, then it needs to feed into our daily lives. Worship has never meant simply getting together to sing sacred songs and celebrate sacred rituals. True Christian worship has always been marked by obedience to God in daily life. This does not mean that everyone has to be a monk or a full-time Christian minister – but we are all called to serve God every day in the ordinary things of life.

With young people this aspect of worship translates very easily into their own search for what they want to do with their lives. Every teenager is faced with the question of a job and a career. These questions need to be seen as a right and proper place to learn to worship God in their calling in life. In traditional Christian language this is the issue of vocation, that is, the belief that God has a calling for each one of us in whatever sphere this may be. And this sense of serving God through a vocation needs to be a part of worship if the Christian faith is to be seen as anything more than just an emotional buzz which you get in a church service. A church service needs to reflect our work lives as much as our work lives need to reflect what we get up to in church.

One definition of worship popular in Catholic circles is "the people's work". In our experience in JOY, setting up an alternative worship service is a lot of work. Each service involves about twenty people working for two weeks before the service in small groups on the music, the prayers, the visuals and the talk. On the day of the service we start work at about 3.30pm to get the whole thing set up and we shut the doors of the church at about 11pm. But when we work together to create the elements of the service and get the building ready we are in fact worshipping. This is an aspect of worship that we are only just starting to experience, but it is very rich indeed. Not only does it foster deep working relationships, but it also draws on the lives of a number of people. In this way the community element of what we are doing is brought into the church service and offered as part of our worship to God. Our everyday lives can be reflected on together and transformed by the power of God's Spirit in our act of worship. This communal aspect of worship will be explored in greater depth in the next two chapters.

NOTES

1. Taken from *The Little Flowers of St Francis*, p52.
2. For more on this see Walter Brueggeman, *Israel's Praise*, p11.

7 · Community

Worship and community go together. Community, of course, is a loaded word. My wife and I lived in community for six years so I know what I'm talking about! The problem is that everyone who uses the word seems to mean something different by it. Despite this I am convinced that the idea of community must be high on our agenda if we want to be successful in creating alternative worship.

One-off eventitis

In the world of Christian youth work there is a tendency to rely upon occasional large get-togethers to provide exciting and relevant worship. As well as the regular feasts of Spring Harvest and Greenbelt there are the touring celebrations which visit a number of towns and cities pulling crowds of young people from a wide area. These events obviously have their place, but we cannot ignore the effect they have on any attempt by a local group to get a new service off the ground.

One of the most damaging effects of what I would call "eventitis" (a disease caused by too many large events) is that we tend to feel inadequate after we have been to them. We look at the band with their big P.A. system and realize we would never be able to afford their gear even if we could learn to play as well! Then there are the massive video screens and high tech "mass media" style presentations. There's no way that the local church can finance such things.

If you are starting to feel this way then *beware*, you may be suffering from the first stages of "eventitis". If you are not treated you will slowly deteriorate into the kind of church leader who gets involved in local worship events. In this early stage of the disease all sorts of spectacular plans and equipment and celebrity guests are got together and booked in the belief that they will attract "them". By "them" of course we mean young people. By "them" we mean a group we know about, but we have failed to consult or involve in our planning in any significant way. When the event we have planned happens, the net result may well look like a real success. Lots of people will turn up and worship God, some may even become Christians, but when all the gear has been packed away and the after-event buzz has started to fade there is an aching emptiness. If we pause to reflect we will start to realize that this emptiness comes from our need for deeper, more significant relationships. We know that these sorts of relationships are usually built in the local church but our experience of running an event is nearly always much more exciting than whatever is happening locally. For the extreme sufferer of "eventitis" the solution is to run another event. But for those seeking a cure the way forward is much more challenging. It's called community.

Growing together

If alternative worship is ever to be anything other than an "event" high on our list of priorities must be the need to build a Christian community. What community will mean exactly will depend a great deal on your own situation. The rest of this chapter describes how in the early days of JOY we wrestled with some of these issues. I don't make any great claims about what we have achieved, but hope our experience may prompt ideas which can be developed elsewhere.

1. *Just friends*

JOY started when a number of different friendship groups got together to plan a service for Greenbelt Festival[1]. In my work with young people I had begun to see a pattern emerge over the years where young people who had become Christians on our evangelistic holiday were failing to find a permanent home in the local churches. We had already established our weekly worship sessions for young Christians but this was not meeting the needs of those who had been Christians for over a year. Worship sessions aimed primarily at those who had newly found faith lacked the challenge to commitment which needs to grow in every disciple.

The chance to move on to something more like a church came when a group from St Aldate's Church in Oxford who were starting to experiment with rave worship got in touch with us. The group was made up of students who were regular worshippers at that church but some of them had already experienced alternative worship in places like St Thomas Crookes in Sheffield. JOY has grown from a coming together of these two different groups, students and local teenagers.

Not surprisingly given the difference between the two groups there was a great deal of tension and suspicion to overcome. At first we did not discuss the sorts of worship that we expected. We spent some considerable time talking with each other and spending informal time in each other's company. We resolved, very early on, that when we started to run worship services the focus of our activity would not be "them", it would be "us". It would be an expression of our ideas, our creativity and our life together as a group. While we would be very open to people coming along and joining in with the service or even with our planning sessions, we would never end up putting on a show. We were meeting together to worship.

2. *Risky business*
Very early on we ran into problems and conflict in our group. The students and their friends from St Aldate's had a real problem with the way the local teenagers behaved and spoke. Most of the young people involved in planning the service smoked, and some of the students found this hard to reconcile

with their idea of Christian behaviour. Like most people in their area the young people would ordinarily use swear words as part of their fairly colourful vocabulary. To hear young people talking about God as "bloody amazing" took some getting used to, and some students found it offensive. The young people also had a tendency to be highly critical of the Church and especially of Church leaders. In fact to this day if someone says something which strikes the group as a bit pious it is greeted by cries of "St Aldate's!" In short to the Christians who were more used to a church setting, these young people did not look right.

The students were made even more uncomfortable by the way the teenagers spoke about God. There was a freshness and an openness about religious experience and the hassles of living the Christian life which sometimes left the more educated and articulate students somewhat in awe of the young people. When people like Stu, Tom, Andy and Wilson shared their experience of God the students could not help but be impressed. They also felt uncomfortable because it meant the young people could not be totally written off as being unChristian.

The teenagers faced with Oxford students for the first time found it a challenge not to dismiss them as being total "prats" or "geeks". The students did not dress right and they tended to get bogged down in ideas and theories. When they prayed they seemed to use words and phrases which were alien to the young people. Yet here were students willing to get to know them and spend time with them. Slowly, respect and friendships began to grow and the young people began to see that the church background of some of the students made them a very valuable spiritual resource. Many of the students were also skilled in the area of art work and one of them was a DJ.

The result was a very creative and energetic community born out of the two groups, yet precisely for these reasons it was a risky business. In part this risk involved moving out of the safe assumptions of your group of friends and beginning to realize that other groups have a great deal to offer. Getting to the point of admitting this was very difficult, and we are still wrestling with this issue. In fact it would be less than honest if I didn't admit that some of us spent a good deal of our energy trying to change the others and convince them we were right. There have been some stormy conflicts over the use of drugs and issues related to sex. We have needed to come to agreement over the personal lifestyles of those involved in leading worship and this has been very tough at times. Some of us found these issues too demanding and painful and had to step aside for a while. We have made mistakes in sorting out some of these things and at times those of us in positions of authority have been a bit heavy-handed. But we have started to learn how to work together on these areas and our commitment to building community has continued and remains at the heart of our worship.

3. *Naturally friends*
One of the strengths of the group was that we were made up of a number of small but very committed friendship groups. For many it was already a normal part of their lives to meet together regularly for social activities. This meant that the group had a strong network of informal contact. If we had hassles then someone was there to talk to and if we felt excited about something then we had a natural group with whom we could celebrate. As we sought to become a community or a fellowship who worshipped together, many of the functions of a normal church fellowship group were already in operation before we started. All we had to do was build on the natural networks that already existed. However this was not as simple as it may appear.

4. *Who's in and who's out?*
In seeking to become a worshipping community we soon realized we would have to create some sort of shared value system which could determine who was part of the group and

who was not. In a friendship group it probably doesn't matter much what people believe, it may even be that members of the same group will have different attitudes to moral issues. The concept of what is "right" and what is "wrong" in a friendship group is usually a matter for negotiation or debate.

Some very thorny issues soon arose. One of the first was to do with who led the worship services. We began to see that people who took an up-front role in the worship needed to reflect Christian values in their lifestyle because we were holding services in a normal church. Soon we were in conflict with each other about the rights and wrongs of taking drugs or of sex outside of marriage. Building a community involves working together on tough and challenging issues and this demands a great deal of trust and commitment on the part of everyone concerned.

I don't think we have sorted this one out as yet, but our experience so far has led me to feel very strongly that two contrasting attitudes need to be held in tension when working on these kinds of questions. The first is that how we behave as Christians is extremely important, but some people will always put themselves outside the group by refusing to wrestle with their own personal lifestyles. It is a mistake to soften the challenge of the faith in order to keep someone inside the group. The other contrasting attitude is the belief that God is working on people in his own very individual and personal way. We are all sinners and God is dealing with different areas of our lives all of the time. In these circumstances it would be wrong to pick on one issue (like sex) and make that the only measure to judge who should be "in" and who should be "out" of the group. These two attitudes need to be kept in a creative balance as we try to work towards the kind of community life that God is calling us to.

5. *Step by step*
Our service JOY happens every other week in one of the local Anglican churches. That sounds fairly straightforward, but

even in this short sentence there are a whole host of problems!
The first and most obvious problem is the Anglican church bit
(I will deal with that in some detail in the next chapter), but
here I want to talk about how an informal group of people starts
to move towards the formality of a regular Sunday worship
slot.

The first problem we encountered was that the community
feel of the group and the demand of producing something every
other week are not easily compatible. Problems come up which
totally take over the atmosphere of the group. It might be that
someone who is down to take part in the service has just split
up with his girlfriend or perhaps been given a hard time by his
parents over some issue. These problems have to be sorted out
for not only are they important in themselves but they also tend
to affect everyone else in the group. If a young person is feeling
low the mood is often picked up by other people. Bad feelings
can hang like a black cloud over the whole group. In these
circumstances putting on a service in front of a bunch of people
may be the last thing the group wants to do, but because we
have organized ourselves to run a service every other week we
can't just junk it when we want to.

Sorting out these sorts of problems can be very time-
consuming, especially when you need to rehearse some tricky
bit of music for a service which is a few hours away! Frustration
over the artistic standard of what someone is doing can very
easily cloud insight into why they are singing off key or
mumbling into the microphone or arguing with anyone who
speaks to them! Young people do face occasional emotional
crises. If the young person who has offered to speak at the
service is chucked by his girlfriend that afternoon, what do you
do? It's at times like these that our only way forward has been
to get together and pray. In fact we learned very early on that
we needed to leave a good deal of time for people to pray and
get into the right mood, both with God and with each other,
if the service was going to go alright. Any problems and
tensions can be sorted out at this time. Even so, the tension

between the "group feel" and the demands of preparing for a fast approaching service is a tricky one to handle.

6. *Everybody's doing it*

Right from the start of JOY we have always had a strong belief that participation by as many young people as possible was at the heart of what were are about. This starts in the area of decision making (see the next chapter) but it also extends into as much involvement by as many people as possible in the services. We try to make space for different people to take up-front leadership roles. This includes the people who preach and sort out the prayers, as well as those who do the music and the visual sides. A typical JOY service will involve twenty or more people working in different areas. One of the ways in which we are alternative is that there is plenty of opportunity for people to exercise their creative gifts in the services. This high level of involvement means that they feel that what happens is "theirs". We don't put on worship for young people – we create it with them.

Getting people to take an active part in the worship has its drawbacks. Things tend not to be very slick, people forget when they are meant to preach, people stumble over their lines, sometimes the unexpected happens but more often the expected doesn't happen! To the outsider this may all seem a little strange, but it stems from our belief in the community feel of our worship. We are all there to have a go at leading worship. We don't rely on experts to do things for us and so at times what happens has an amateur, home grown flavour.

The fact that young people participate fully in the worship is very important. One Sunday one of the young people who usually plays guitar in the band got up to do the sermon. He wasn't used to preaching and he was fairly nervous about the whole thing, his talk was full of "errs" and "umms" and mumbled things that most of us missed. But what he said, in his own style, had a power to move people. Another young person I chatted to after the service who had come to JOY for the first time said he was really impressed that someone had got up and talked in an ordinary and everyday way about Jesus. Despite the obviously "amateur" approach to preaching, he was able to identify with what was said and the person who said it, precisely because he wasn't any great shakes at preaching.

Certainly our service sometimes lacks professionalism, but because we are a group of people who care about each other it doesn't much matter if things go wrong. This communal aspect to the worship is in fact its strength. Of course every now and then we discover new and exciting gifts in the group which would never have emerged without the space for people to get up there and have a go. Most people who are part of JOY are excited about the opportunities to be creative and be involved in doing something new and different.

7. *Planning together*

The fact that so many people are involved in the creation of our services means that we do need to exercise some care over the kinds of things that happen. Every week we meet to plan the service as a group. These planning meetings give us all a chance to hear what is going to be said in the talk and the prayers as well as look at some of the visuals. The group exercises its own censorship. If something seems to be out of order or not in tune with the feel of the service then we are free to say so at this meeting. In this way we can make sure that decisions about the service can be taken together.

A work of the Spirit

Christian community cannot be created by our own efforts, however good they may be. Whatever we achieve happens because of God's activity amongst us by his Spirit.

This factor in our life together is both frustrating and comforting. It is frustrating because we don't know what God is going to do, things turn up unexpectedly, people change and grow or get challenged and move out of the main stream for a while. The work of the Spirit amongst us means that we are always having to react to a new and creative situation. There is at times a feeling that things are a bit out of control. In fact I am constantly amazed at the way that God brings things about in our group which we did not plan for or even expect! The communal life which goes along with an alternative worship service needs to have this "organic" and natural feel because it is based on the informal friendships young people build in the everyday run of things. This means that it will always feel like uncertain ground because it is a fluid situation, but this is where God's challenge can be most effective. People on the move can be inspired to new things much more easily than those who are rooted to the same spot. And discipleship is about following Christ.

There is always a sense in which the whole enterprise is in God's hands and not in ours – and this is its strength. We need to hang on to the belief that this community has come into being because God has decided that it should. Our role is simply to recognize where God is at work among us and depend on his action in our midst. That does not mean that we don't make plans or try to organize things as best we can, but it does mean that we are always resting in his hands – and from where I'm standing that is extremely comforting.

NOTE

1. The name JOY was originally used by the students from St Aldate's for their raves. When the new group was formed we decided to stick with it.

8 · Leadership

Communities need organization. Without it everyone gets confused and fed up, and the worship service won't come together.

One approach to organization is to try to get everything sorted out right from the start. I remember one group meeting where I drew lots of boxes and arrows on a piece of paper to express how we should structure JOY. It was greeted with howls of disagreement and objections. "We don't want that sort of thing," they all said, "we just want to let it grow." They were right and I put my piece of paper away.

This incident highlights the role of leadership and decision-making in running new forms of worship. Leaders face a dilemma: on the one hand we want to see things getting going, but we also realize that we can very easily take things over, stifling creativity. Working with young people to write a worship song, for instance, may well take a good deal of time. It is tempting to go ahead and write it yourself. But I have found that this kind of "go it alone" leadership style does not build real alternative worship. It is created by young people but not for them.

Another factor is that young people need time to develop the skill of handling regular responsibility. They need to learn to be leaders. Many is the time when a young person has merrily offered to do something like get the church ready for the service, or make sure everyone knows about a meeting, and in the event they have not done it. As adults we know what it is to make mistakes or find that we have taken on too much. This often happens among teenagers and indeed it could be argued that it forms an important part of their learning process.

Running a church is an arduous business and young people need sensitive and careful leadership if the project will ever get under way. My own experience is that this kind of leadership is far from easy, but it will nearly always involve the development of a team of older helpers who can work together on a worship service. Within this team a number of different functions and gifts will need to be worked out. This chapter gives an insight into some of the lessons we have learned so far in JOY.

Being there to listen

While it is important that leaders have some sort of vision for the future and are able to share their ideas with others, it is vital that this vision grows from an intimate relationship with the group that are going to create the worship. As leaders we need to put a high priority on listening to the young people themselves. In the first instance this will involve spending a good deal of time with the group in situations where they feel comfortable.

Listening is hard work because to understand other people's lives and perspectives is very demanding. It is only when we have a sensitivity to these perspectives that we will be able to be a leader who can help the group develop its own style of worship. Of course we need not feel that we can never ever say anything or suggest any ideas, in fact the main point of listening is so that we can help in the creative process. But it is only when we are close to the situation of the young people that we will be best equipped to suggest ideas and ways forward in the light of our knowledge of the group. We also need to be listeners who are open to what God is saying to the group.

In the early stages of the development of JOY I often found that my role was to sum up what had been said in a discussion and feed my reflections back to the group to see if what I thought was being expressed was also shared by everyone else.

This kind of listening means that as a leader I was simply helping the group to come to a common mind about a particular issue. I think of this process as a way of seeking out what the Spirit is saying through the group and my role as a leader is to try to put some shape to this. On other occasions there has been a need for one person to express what God is saying to the group, but this has not been our usual experience.

Sharing decisions

In the early days of JOY most decisions were made at a meeting to which everyone involved was invited. We all felt it important that we could have a say in what was going on and raise ideas and objections. At first it was very hard to get this group to make decisions. Some of the issues that arose seemed a bit remote from most people's experience, and some quite frankly seemed boring. So many people getting together to make decisions did tend to be a bit rowdy and many was the time when it seemed more fun to crack a few jokes or jump on someone and tickle them than to talk about setting up a service! Yet it was part of our plan to allow space for all of the young people involved to have a say in what we were going to do. This was vital to the eventual shape not only of our worship, but of our whole group organization and feel. Looking back now, young people say they very much value the fact that they have the power to affect what happens at every level of our life together. But I must say that achieving this kind of power sharing has not been easy and it is a struggle that gets more and more difficult as time goes on and things get more complicated.

After a year of corporate decision-making we decided that we needed to have a smaller group taking responsibility for JOY. This group works with and for the larger group. In other words we want to keep some kind of forum within which everyone can have a say in the running of the service. But at the same time we need to have a small "executive" type group which can act more quickly and provide a more stable environment for what goes on. We elected six people who would be "where the buck stops" in JOY.

We came to this point because decision-making in such a large group did not work very well. We found that letting everyone have a say about everything, while very important in the early days, became very cumbersome as time went on. One reason for this was that JOY had grown significantly in numbers. Instead of ten or twenty we now had fifty or more people at each planning meeting. At first we tried to split up into smaller working groups to discuss things, but eventually the size of the group defeated us. We also found that making decisions was one thing, getting them to become reality was quite another.

Making things happen

Leaders don't just take decisions. They actually make things happen. For leadership is the ability to work with a group of people to create something. One example of this in JOY is in the whole area of social action. Early on we all decided to give away a percentage of the money we received to needy projects in the local community. In researching this we found that many people needed practical help more than they needed money. So over the last year a group of three or four women have started to get involved in caring for the homeless and the handicapped. At first they did this on their own, then they began to invite other JOY members along to help. This kind of leadership was very effective as practical social action was able to grow out of the decision-making of the group. Helping a group of people achieve what they want to achieve is one of the main functions of a leader in alternative worship.

When JOY first got under way there was a feeling in the group that planning a whole service was a bit too mind-boggling and difficult. At that time it was tempting simply to organize everyone and tell them what they should do, but as far as I was concerned this would defeat the object of the exercise – allowing young people to have the power to create worship. Instead of taking total control I decided that the best way to operate was to create a simple structure for the service. By dividing it into small bite-sized portions we were better able to be creative on each section of the service because it was much more manageable.

Our simple structure went like this: Introduction, Bible bit, Confession, music, prayers, Peace, Communion. At that first meeting I put each of these general headings on the top of a few pieces of paper and put them in a rough order. Then we brainstormed ideas for each area. This process gave the young people small areas which they could easily imagine and get to grips with. Having sorted out each individual area we then found that the service slotted into place very easily. This approach to leadership meant that I was simply making sure, first, that the service got planned, but second, that everyone had the chance to contribute to what was going on.

Growing leaders

Getting JOY up and running has in effect been a slow process of encouraging people to have a go at things so that over a period of time they can slowly discover what their gifts and abilities are. This means that we regularly get new people doing the prayers or the talks in services. We encourage as many people as possible to take part. For instance, we may ask them to experiment with leading meetings or to sort out the slides and the music for the services. What has been amazing has been how many under-used and undiscovered gifts there are in any one group of young people. Paul's message about the body of Christ and each of us having gifts has shown itself time and time again to be a true picture of the Church in our experience. Gradually more and more people have joined the group and slowly they have begun to share the responsibility for the various aspects of the service and the fellowship groups which we run.

At first this approach to developing leadership was very taxing. Often people would say that they would do something and then bottle out at the last minute. One famous fellowship group, planned by a young person who will remain nameless, simply consisted of him saying the word "Armageddon". There we were with no Bible passages, no discussion material, in fact with no guidance at all other than this one word and we were expected to spend a whole evening of fellowship together! Needless to say we have been on a very sharp learning curve with our leadership for a while now! The most important lesson that I have learned is not to panic. In the short term the group will try to help out with the problem. At our Armageddon meeting other people in the group realized that things needed some helping along and started to contribute and make the best of it. The group will throw up its own leadership over a period of time as people show themselves to be good at some things and bad at others.

I have found that my own role in the evolution of JOY has changed quite considerably. In the first instance it was my job to get the service up and running. In the very early days I had to be at every meeting and give advice on almost every aspect of the service. Very quickly, within a matter of weeks, people started to need me a good deal less. Partly this was because they had now been involved in one or two services from beginning to end, and they found it much more easy to act as helpers and leaders when they knew roughly what was expected of them. Within about six months my presence at planning meetings and even at the services themselves was not really required. The group had created its own competent leaders who were able to run the services themselves.

Creating an environment in which natural leaders can grow is not easy. In the first place we need to make space for them to lead, by allowing them to take responsibility for things. Sometimes we have to be willing for them to learn "on the job''. That means that they will have to make some mistakes. At the same time there is a real need for those who are a little older to support the young people in what they are trying to do.

One way that we have tried to do this is by making sure that each area of JOY has a mix of young people and older people working together on it. Where a young person takes responsibility for a major part of the service, e.g. the talk, we will make sure that someone helps them, perhaps talking it through and giving them a chance to practise it in front of a small audience. In this way we are able to nurture the gifts and abilities of the group.

Learning to delegate

It would be misleading to see JOY as just an exercise in creative chaos! From the start we organized ourselves into teams which worked on the various aspects of the service. We have a small group which organizes the slides and pictures for each service, a group which sets up the church and puts everything back where it should be, a group which writes the music and performs it, and so on. From the beginning it was clear that there needed to be a way to oversee everything that was being planned. When we started to run two services every month the problems seemed to just get bigger and bigger. Our solution was to set up a small group which was co-ordinated by one of the leaders, the heroic Anna Hall. This small group had a floating membership depending on who was involved in planning the next service. Jobs were allocated and then people would go back to the various teams and start to work on their particular area.

This process has thrown up the need for young people to be free to drift in and out of positions of responsibility. The bonus is that it spreads the load and gives a larger number of people a chance to contribute to the service. But it is also important to allow young people the space to go through their own personal problems if they need to or simply to have the freedom to get a bit enthusiastic at times without having to bear too much of the load. At the same time Anna's role has been vital because it means we always have a safe and secure reference point for everybody and at least one person knows what is going on. In any one service there may be as many as twenty or thirty people contributing, mostly behind the scenes, but they all need to know what they are meant to be doing.

We have tried to encourage leadership throughout the various teams in JOY. One way that we have done this is by encouraging the adults involved to work in one area with a group of young people. These adults can bear the load of responsibility for running their particular part of the service while at the same time helping the young people to play as full a role as they feel they can. Running a service every other week is hard work. The young people in JOY are extremely enthusiastic, but they find regular long-term responsibility can be too much for them at times. The adults in the group, therefore, create a dependable structure for JOY which means that the whole weight of the service does not fall on a small group of teenagers. They are also there to exercise leadership by helping the young people to express themselves in worship.

Dealing with the big-wigs

JOY takes place in an Anglican church, and this means that there are vicars and church authorities to be dealt with. As a leader I have been a bit of a go-between, talking to the church leaders and smoothing the way for the easy growth and development of the service. In the early days this meant that I had to contact various church leaders and get their okay for what we were planning. I also made sure there were a number of different options open to us when the time came for us to find a home in a local church. This meant setting up formal meetings with local clergy and a bit of politics behind the scenes to make sure that what the group was heading for was in fact possible. It was also important to look out for potential flash points between the church and the group and try to steer things in a way which would keep the majority of people happy.

One example of this is the fact that we have a Communion as one of our main services. Being a part of the Anglican set-up meant we needed to make sure that our plans were acceptable from the Church's point of view. My own knowledge of the Church and of the young people meant that I could make sure that we kept ourselves out of too much deep water. Having said this we have pushed the boundaries as far as we could within the legal framework of our denomination.

The Church from its point of view needed to feel that what was going on was safe. The local clergy needed to know that there was someone in the group who was taking ultimate responsibility and to whom they could express their fears and reservations. It was also important that trust was built up right from the start with an adult they felt they could deal with. We have also tried to formalize our contact with the local church by setting up a pastoral reference group where our leaders and the local clergy and other lay people could get together and review what was happening and set down some markers for the future. This meeting gives a forum for an exchange of insights and ideas between the young people and the local church without setting up any formal managerial structures. As time goes on, however, we may need to make these relationships more formal, especially if we decide to employ a full-time pastoral worker.

A word about priests

From the start JOY has wanted to be very firmly rooted in a church context. This has been for a number of reasons, high among them the desire that a traditional church be a welcoming place for young people and the culture which they create. There has also been a strong feeling that being part of an established church enables us to be in a creative relationship with a rich Christian tradition. The positive attitude of the local priest at St Mary and John Church in Oxford has been very important in the development of our worship, but first and foremost has been his willingness to learn from the young people what is best for JOY.

Because we meet in an Anglican church as part of that church's weekly round of worship, the priest has ultimate responsibility for what goes on. Fr Martin Flatman, our priest, has been very helpful in letting us get on with planning the services ourselves. His role has never been to sanction or censure what we get up to − apart from the odd minor abuse of the church's property! The young people in JOY for their part took to Father Martin straight away. He was enthusiastic and welcoming and they responded to his warmth: "He's a cool dude." The fact that Martin was a priest was less important than the fact that he was a good guy. But in the long term his role as the parish priest has been very important.

JOY also has a link with St Aldate's Church in the centre of the town. David MacInnes, its rector, and members of his staff together with Father Martin are regularly present at our services. By their presence they are being a visible link with the Anglican church. In effect they are saying, "This might not look like it, but it is part of our church." This is one of the most important gifts that the church can give to the young people who are taking part in the worship, because it is a tangible and human expression that we belong. We are not some orphaned off-shoot. We are not a separate fellowship or organization. We are a legitimate expression of the Anglican Church's life. By being with us in our worship and celebrating Communion with us Martin and David are not allowing the church to write us off as a strange sect. People like the bishop (who fully supports what we are up to) and the other church authorities have to reckon with us and come to terms with what we are doing.

The priest is also important in the Anglican Communion

because he is seen as the means by which the sacraments of
Christ's Church are given to us all. In JOY we have always
tried to emphasize an evangelical commitment within a
sacramental framework, upholding the clear teaching of the
Gospel alongside more symbolic representations such as the
sacraments.

In the Anglican Church only the priest can celebrate
Communion.

Some may feel that truly alternative worship should be free
of the denominational restrictions of an established Church.
To my mind though, a separate fellowship of young people
is not an option[1]. In the first place they need the tradition of
the older Church to react against and be creative with.
Secondly, the history of separate congregations is not very
inspiring since they often quickly lose their reforming ideals
and become much more stuck-in-the-mud than the
congregations they left in the first place. Accepting the
discipline of an established church does not mean, however,
that we cannot work for change. As one young person said
in the talk at the very first JOY service, ''JOY is part of the
Anglican Church but it is embarrassed about it.'' It is this kind
of sentiment that makes us want to see change, and one
symbolically significant example is in the area of priesthood.

We confine the priest's role in our services only to those
sacramental parts of the service for which he is absolutely
necessary. He takes centre stage only for the consecration of
the bread and the wine. The servant nature of the priesthood
is highlighted here. He serves the young people by allowing
himself to take the back seat, and then as a minister of Christ's
Church he serves us by celebrating Communion. There is a
symbolism here which strikes to the very heart of what we are
trying to do by growing worship from the context of young
people. It shows the Church blessing our creativity, our life,
and our energy. There is no attempt to control or to take an
inappropriately authoritative line with young people. Instead
we see the priest's role as that of a servant, and it has to be

said that when we are moving chairs at the end of the service Martin and the curate, Mike, are always there doing a share of the work and they are nearly always the last ones to leave. This also speaks volumes about the church's commitment to JOY and to the young people involved with it.

NOTE

1. I argue for this approach in much more detail in *Youth Culture and the Gospel*, chapter 15.

Part Two

Doing Worship

Part 2 is about the practicalities of organizing alternative worship. Each chapter deals with a different part of a normal service at JOY, giving a few general comments followed by some practical examples.

Alternative worship is multi-media in nature and so along with chapters on prayer and music there are also sections on the use of pictures and dance in worship.

Central to alternative worship is the fact that young people are involved in creating it. So this section of the book is not a do-it-yourself alternative worship kit. The examples I have included are there as a guide to your own planning and creativity. This doesn't mean that some of the ideas might not work in your church. They might do, but they will be much more powerful if they have been adapted by your own group for their needs.

9 · The Elements of Worship

I used to switch off whenever anyone used the term "liturgy". It sounded churchy and dull. But the word started to have new meaning for me when I learned that "liturgy" actually means "people's work".

I realized that liturgy was about the way God expects us to work at serving him in worship. Of course "people's work" is a term which includes the way we live our everyday lives, but this chapter concentrates on how we shape a worship service. It looks at the practical ways to create not just the content of our worship – the songs or the words we say together – but also the atmosphere in which we worship.

Creating a place for worship

Our service takes place in a traditional Anglican church. Luckily the seats are all movable so our first job on arrival is to move all the chairs to create a large open space in the middle of the church. This is a lot of hard work, but it means that people are free to move about during the service. This is important because dancing to rave music needs a lot of space, and also because from time to time we invite people to take part in symbolic acts (see Chapter 12 for more on this) which usually means that everyone has to move around a bit. We scatter the church's kneelers around the floor so that there is at least something soft to sit on, and groups will be able to sit together in much more intimate ways than rows of chairs would allow. In churches with fixed pews there is sometimes enough space at the front or at the back to hold a small service.

Our next job involves stringing up a number of massive

white sheets all around the space we have created. We use these sheets as giant screens onto which we project pictures and images throughout the service (Chapter 15 gives more detail). Once again this involves a lot of effort as brave people climb up to the top of the church and attach the screens to the pillars and a great deal of time is spent getting hold of slide projectors and getting them to work just right. Incidentally you don't need to spend a great deal of money on this area of the service. We have managed to create some truly spectacular visual effects with just a few borrowed slide machines. When all the screens are filled with the pictures projected on to them, the congregation are surrounded by colourful images. Each of the sheets becomes a wall of light so that we sit in a square surrounded on every side by pictures.

What is amazing is how the pictures on the screens are able to affect the mood of people worshipping in quite powerful ways, so much so that when people first arrive there is a definite hesitation on their part to enter the worship area because the sense of God's presence is so powerful.

Sounds and smells

We use both prerecorded music and a live band so setting up the sound equipment is fairly technical. We try to position the speakers all around the area where people are worshipping, so that the music surrounds the space. We are anxious not to make the band a focus of the worship so the centre of attention is either the screen on which the words of the songs are projected, or if it is a Communion service then the altar is placed centrally. We make a big thing of the altar because of our emphasis on the Communion in our worship. In JOY young people hear the Word of God, but they are also invited to experience God's presence with them in the sacraments. The altar is a visible sign of this presence with us. We have made a psychedelic cloth which we put over the front of the altar. For one service we placed on it a cross made from lots of pieces of scrap metal and junk, created in a workshop by a group of young people. Using something that a group has made in a worship is another way to involve young people.

When people come into the church the first thing they hear is loud dance music, which we always play for about fifteen minutes before the service starts. Just like the pictures on the screens, the music has the effect of creating a special atmosphere. This gives a sense of a place which is full of life and energy, a stimulating environment where the readiness to worship God is encouraged. The music slowly starts to touch them and creates a sense of expectancy. As more people arrive some will start to move around and dance. We see this as an important part of creating "a place to worship" with sight and sound combining to direct our attention towards the service which is about to start.

We have also found that incense can help in creating a special environment for worship. Our church uses incense every Sunday so there is no problem with filling the place with noxious fumes! Usually we simply burn the incense throughout the service, but once or twice one of the older members of the regular St Mary and John congregation has waved the stuff around in a censor (or handbag on fire as we jokingly refer to it). Once again the main reason for burning incense is to create an environment which stimulates people in as many ways as possible to turn to God in prayer and worship.

The House of God

One of our songs sums up what we try to create in preparing a place for worship. Part of it goes like this:

> This is the House of God
> This is the gate of heaven
> God Almighty is here.

The House of God is a holy place where God chooses to come and meet us. Through pictures, music, incense, and the symbolism of the altar people become aware that they have entered a special place where something incredibly unusual is about to happen: God through his Spirit is going to touch us. One way to symbolize this presence of God is by burning candles. Jesus is the light of the world and the candles are a visible reminder of the fact that he is there with us. Sometimes these are only on the altar, but at other times we have covered large areas of the floor with small night lights often in the form of a giant cross. Be warned, however, cleaning up the wax after the service is a bit of a pain! But this attention to the environment in which we worship would be empty if we didn't also recognize that the House of God is crucially the people who have gathered together.

Before we start our service everyone involved meets to pray. We want to be ready for what we are about to do and we want to invite God to be present in powerful ways among us. This prayer is a key element in creating the atmosphere. When the core group who are leading the service have a sense of harmony and expectancy this usually transmits itself to everyone else who comes to the service. We have taken this idea and applied it to various parts of the way we run the service.

The first way we try to help people catch the mood of those running the service is by encouraging those regular members of JOY who are not "up front" to scatter themselves around the edges of the congregation. This means that they are able to welcome people informally. We find that many hesitate before they move into the worship space. If a large crowd gathers on the edge and looks onto an empty space this can make for bad vibes, and they become inhibited about getting into the worship because they feel self-conscious. To avoid this kind of goldfish bowl feeling we encourage people to move into the centre, or to sit on one of the few seats we provide for the wrinklies (our pet name for those older people at JOY who find it hard to sit on the floor). With a few people spread around the edges of the worship space we find that the whole congregation warms up and starts to enter into the worship more quickly. As the service gets going people who are visiting the service for the first time can take their cues from the regulars. During the songs the regulars are more likely to jig around a bit or sing the songs with some confidence and newcomers nearby soon start to relax and join in.

Another interesting way the regulars set the scene is by dancing behind the screens so that they create shadows. When people first arrive at the service they see these figures in the background worshipping God in a very free way and this adds to the sense that something exciting is about to happen.

Planning a service

Usually a number of different groups of people work on the different elements of the service. They are encouraged to be creative with their part of the service, and this means that it is very important to communicate together so that ideas don't clash or repeat themselves. At the start of each term we meet together to decide on a theme for the next group of services. So far we have covered aspects of the Christian life like faith and forgiveness and a whole series on the Ten Commandments. These themes have been chosen by the group because they dealt with issues we were facing at that particular time.

Having chosen a theme and given people a while to think up a few ideas we get together and brainstorm each service and its various elements. This can be a very creative time where people start to spark off ideas in each other. One person comes up with an idea for drama, perhaps, and this sets another group thinking about visuals or music. In this way enthusiasm is generated for the service which can be carried into the next phase, where we work out in the teams the way each part of the service interprets the theme.

Having said this, however, there is a great need for an overview of the whole shape of the service. Here are a few of the areas we have learned to bear in mind:

1. *Word and symbol*

Incense, pictures and the sacraments of the Church make us open to more intangible or "mystical" approaches to God. This sensitivity needs to be held in balance with a commitment to clear teaching. In every service we make sure that the Bible is either read aloud or the relevant story acted out in a dramatic form. Someone talks about the message for that Sunday in clear and understandable terms.

Striking a balance between the symbolic and straight teaching is very important because it means that we consciously try to convey the wholeness of the Gospel which is relevant to body, mind and spirit. We all need to think about God in clear objective terms as well as experience his touch subjectively through the use of music or pictures. This balance is very well modelled by the traditional Anglican Communion service with its emphasis on Word and Sacrament. For this reason we have two services each month. One is based on the Communion Service, the other is left more open to allow for more lengthy teaching or prayer and meditation, though in this service too we keep a balance between word and symbol by including some kind of action which complements the teaching. This could simply be the lighting of a candle but it always attempts to provide a balance by echoing the teaching in symbolic form.

2. *Movement and stillness*

Dance is an important part of our service, but we are also concerned to make space for people to quieten themselves before God. Both movement and stillness have a place in worship. In fact we have found that a rapid contrast between an energetic dance track and a time where people meditate can work very well. We use a number of different ways to help us in our stillness. Sometimes we sit in total silence, and here it helps to have something on which we can focus our attention – a picture or candles. We have also used quiet music as an aid to meditation. However the balance between movement and stillness is achieved, the two complement each other very well and contribute to the rhythm and flow of the service.

3. *Who leads?*

In planning a service we try to make sure that a wide variety of people are involved, all offering their own individual gifts and abilities. This is important because those who lead the service to some extent act as representatives of those who worship and this can only work if people are able to relate to those who lead. We get a large number of young people involved in our worship, but we only use those who are committed in their desire to follow Christ in up-front roles. We are also very concerned to endorse the equal ministry of women among us, so in most services we make sure that both men and women lead. Getting this balance was hard at first because the blokes were more pushy and spoke louder in the meetings, but a policy of encouragement of women in leadership roles has helped. I am pleased to see that this attitude has been endorsed by the Anglican Church's decision to ordain women to the priesthood.

4. *A human presence*

We have an emphasis on the technological side of things with slides and music, but we have also learned that people need to have a strong person taking the lead with whom they can identify as the worship progresses.

In the early days we wanted to ensure that the worship flowed with as few interruptions as possible from people introducing the next stage. We wanted a sense of flow and an element of surprise.

One way we achieved this was by projecting all the words used in the service on the screens. This removed the need for books or the problem of it being too dark to read. But we have learned to our cost that a great deal of attention needs to be paid to getting these slides in the right order and the person operating them needs to be on the ball! We have also found that using an OHP creates too much light and spoils the atmosphere. Slides work best. But we find we need to balance the ''cold'' feel of words on a screen with the warmer presence of a worship leader who adds the human elements. The service leader will sometimes encourage people to stand up when a song starts or explain a bit about the theme of the service. Once again a balance needs to be created between the flow of the worship and the need for a few jokes and asides to help relax everyone and reassure them that they are not alone in starting to worship God. People need a safe reference point if they are going to take the risk of entering into worship.

Usually we make sure that at the start someone gets up and says, ''Welcome to JOY, we're glad you have come to this service.'' They can also explain a bit about the way the service works, for instance that all the words to the songs are displayed on the screens and they are free to join in the singing if they want to.

The words we say

In the Anglican Church a service is made up of a whole series of set prayers that are written down in a book. When we came to plan our own Communion service we decided to take a look at the existing service and see what we made of it. The first thing we did was cut most of it out, as we felt it was much too complicated!

The service is made up of a few stages which flow on from one another. These are: Welcome, Word, Confession, Peace, Communion, End. Having established these general areas we then looked at the most basic prayers from the existing service to see if they met our own needs. We decided to stick to the general format for the Communion service because it gave us something to work from. It also meant that the priest could easily relate to what we were doing.

Of course it is not necessary to use the Church of England's pattern for a service and we have experimented with a

Communion Service used in the United Reformed Church. But in both of these situations we were setting up a quite deliberate dialogue between the old tradition of the Church and the language and music of young people. Adapting an existing service sets this up quite nicely. In a Free Church tradition a similar thing could be achieved by using the biblical accounts of the Last Supper in the gospels and in 1 Corinthians chapter 11.

When we looked at the Church of England service in the ASB we found that a few of the prayers made sense and sounded quite good so we kept them in. But one or two of them we felt needed to be changed if we were going to use them. A small group of people got together and, using the original as a guideline, wrote an up-dated version. Here are two examples of our work. The first one is said by everyone right at the start of the service, the second is our form of the Confession.

> Everloving Lord, our hearts are open to you
> And you know all our desires
> We can't hide any secrets from you
> By your Holy Spirit
> Come into us
> Purify our motives and strengthen our minds
> So that we can openly love you
> And worship you
> With the glory and respect
> That is rightfully yours
> Through Jesus Christ your Son. Amen.

> Father, the things we've thought and said and done
> Have let other people down, but most of all
> They've let you down.
> We're sorry for all the times when we've hurt you:
> When we've been forgetful or weak
> Or just because we haven't cared.
> Thank you that through your Son, Jesus Christ,
> We can be forgiven.

Please forgive us for all the things we've done
Which we are ashamed of.
Please help us to start again.

In writing these prayers we tried as far as possible to make the language informal and personal. We wanted prayers which didn't sound too posh or stuffy and that most people could understand straight away. This doesn't mean slang expressions. If the prayers are too up-to-date they will age very quickly, and "trendy" prayers tend to sound hollow and contrived. By keeping to simple everyday speech we feel that we have avoided these problems. Of course each group needs to solve problems in its own way. Here are a few guidelines for your own attempts at creating words to use in worship

1. Keep it brief. Long prayers are boring. Young people very happily say parts of the service together but for this to work well it needs to be short.
2. Keep it simple. Complicated prayers are less powerful than ones which say what they mean clearly and concisely.
3. Make it deep. Young people want to be challenged in church to reach into themselves as well as out to God.
4. Use symbolic language. Words like light, life, love, fire, and water are rich in their imaginative impact. Young people are moved by language which is rich in symbol and meaning.
5. Work in a group. If these prayers are to reflect the interests of your group of young people, involve them in writing them.
6. Use sparingly. Set prayers are good but they need to be supplemented by a variety of other approaches to worship. Young people need to be free to write material for each service. There also needs to be space for visuals, music and drama.

10 · The Word

The Bible needs to be at the heart of any kind of Christian worship. When a large amount of experimentation is going on it is very important that the Bible is a cornerstone on which all the creativity is based. This may sound obvious, but it is in fact a very difficult balance to get right. Too much caution leads to boring worship which lacks a cutting edge, but if there is no concern to keep in touch with the roots of the Christian Gospel the whole thing can lose the spiritual power and life which the Word of God brings to us. It is of utmost importance that what is growing, both at a community level and in the up-front worship, comes out of a willingness to wrestle with the Bible and its message. But this does not mean that we have to follow the patterns which have already been established in the Church. We can discover new ways of doing things.

Learning to learn

Most people learn by doing and then talking about what they have done. The sermon approach to learning is not very effective, because it doesn't allow people to talk through what has been said and integrate it into their own lives and experiences. In most churches too much is expected of the sermon in terms of teaching people about the faith. This does not mean that talks and sermons do not have a place in worship. It is important to spend some time listening to the Bible and thinking about what it says.

In each JOY service there is always a spot which is focused around the Bible but this does not mean that we always have a sermon. We try to vary the ways that we think about God's message. Usually a young person stands up front sharing what they feel God is saying through the Bible passage. They do this in their own way, some talking about their own story in relation to the Bible, others preferring to lead a kind of meditation on the passage. We also vary this with interviews and the use of drama. In all these ways we are not so much trying to offer a sermon slot, we are more concerned to make space for the Bible and God's Word to speak. The important thing is that we focus somehow on God's Word. The sermon is just one way of doing this, but there are other ways which work just as well and in some cases a lot better.

The best way to help people to learn about living the Christian life is in small groups where the Bible can be studied in relation to real life events. In small groups people can go at their own pace and learn in ways that suit their abilities and gifts. People can set their own programme for study and reflection, and there is much more room for discussion and questions. You can talk through your experiences and then listen to what other people have to say and learn from them. For young people this method of learning is, of course, extremely important, because it gives them a chance to "try the Faith on" and see what it looks like. It also avoids the more authoritarian overtones of one older person standing up and telling them what to think and how to act. If everyone is able to have a say and contribute to what is going on, there is a much higher chance that a lively and culturally relevant approach to the Faith will begin to grow.

Learning in the context of worship

In JOY people are already meeting in small groups where informal learning and discussion can take place. This means that when we come to our fortnightly worship service, we are able to concentrate on a few simple points to establish the theme of the service and to challenge people to worship God and carry this worship out into their daily lives. We are not concerned to teach the Christian faith in any systematic or complicated way, because, as I have already said, the best place to do this is in the small groups. We do concentrate very hard on conveying the message of the Bible in the services, but we try to do this in as varied and attractive and accessible a way as we can. Here are a few of the ideas we have come up with to use the Bible in worship and then some thoughts about preaching.

1. *Using the Bible in worship*
a) The most simple way of using the Bible in worship is just to read it! We have found that this approach works extremely well. People expect to hear the Bible read in church and it feels okay. However we try to make sure that what is read is fairly short and not too complicated. If possible the reading should be a story which Jesus told, or a story about Jesus. Young people need to be able to identify with the characters in the Bible passage. Something about the story needs to echo with a situation they have found themselves in. The story of the woman taken in adultery is a good one about sex, Peter's denial of Jesus talks about loyalty and friendship. These two characters in the Bible, like many others, come over as real people who are touched by the fact that Jesus has entered their lives. The Good News Bible is our favoured version to read aloud because it is fairly simple in its use of language.

b) An easy way to liven up a reading and bring it to life for people is to dramatize it. The simplest way to do this is to separate the passage into different parts so that each character in the story is read by a different person. This needs a small amount of rehearsal, but it does make the Bible come alive.

c) Bible readings can be very effective when they are read over a meditative style of music. This might be distracting to some people, but for young people who are used to having music as a constant background to every kind of activity it is often very helpful. Using music in this way means that the flow of the service is not interrupted by stopping for a Bible reading.

The fact that the music carries on gives a strong sense of direction to the service and it also means that when the music stops there is a deliberate reason for it, for example, when the sermon happens and we want everyone focused on that one event. Usually we use pre-recorded music for this, but live music can work just as well. Whatever type of music is used it is very important that the music does not drown out the reader. It also helps if the people reading are fairly happy with speaking into microphones. Once again a bit of rehearsing is needed to make sure that this works well.

d) It is very effective to link the pictures which we project on the screens with the Bible passage which is being read. It is possible to find pictures which exactly match the story so that the Bible passage is illustrated. One way of doing this is to draw cartoons and photograph them. Another way would be to set up a kind of photo story such as you see in teenage magazines. The story of the prodigal son lends itself quite naturally to this approach. Instead of bubbles with words in for dialogue, you could act each of the parts out live as the pictures were shown. An alternative approach is to choose pictures which are in general terms an echo of the rough theme of the reading. This approach works well where the passage deals with big ideas. With John chapter 1, for example, here are some suggested images:

verses 1–5 The world from outer space.
verses 6–7 Early morning sunrise with mist on the fields.
verses 10–13 People walking down the High Street in town.
verse 14 Big smiling face.

For more on the use of pictures in worship see Chapter 15.

e) Bible stories are very effective if they are acted out. We usually update a story and either act it out in full or more usually have some simple drama taking place while someone reads the passage. In one service we acted out the parable of the three servants who are given different amounts of money (Matthew 25: 14–30) using a large circle of candles to represent

what each servant was given to work with. One worked hard
and lit up most of his candles, so did the second, but the one
with the fewest candles just messed about with the hot wax.
This sort of thing can of course be a bit corny, so we try to
make sure that what happens is in tune with the rest of the
service.

Usually material we have written is more successful than
using Christian drama books which are sometimes out of touch
with young people, probably because they reflect the Church
setting which they have grown out of. Material we write
ourselves reflects the interests and language of the young
people. One effective idea is to act out a Bible story behind
screens so that you create a shadow effect. This works well
if the drama is a mime with good background music. If the
acting is clear and full of big gestures then it can be very
powerful. The parable of the prodigal son has a bit of violence
in it and that always works well in shadow theatre. Simple
costumes can be made out of paper or cardboard to create a
more dramatic shadow on the screen, especially big hats. The
young people in JOY like doing this sort of drama because they
can act stupid while remaining hidden behind a screen. They
tend to feel a bit exposed doing the straight sorts of drama.

f) The Bible can also be set to music. On a few occasions we
have taken Psalms or other song passages of the Bible like the
Magnificat and set them to our own times. This can either be
performed to the others, or everyone can join in. Another
simple way to get the words across more clearly is to project
them onto the screens so that people can read the words for
themselves as they are being sung.

2. *Preaching the Word*

Preaching in the context of worship is very powerful. It is one
of the ways God consistently uses to challenge us. Once again
this does not mean doing things in exactly the same way that
the Church has always done them. In fact it is very important
to try to experiment with this part of the service as much as

possible if only to try to keep people interested in what is happening. I try to encourage the attitude that the best things are yet to be done. This attitude, it seems to me, is particularly true of the preaching we are subjected to in church! We try to be as creative as we can with the sermon slot, and as well as having one person standing up front speaking, we vary the format with interviews, testimonies and groups of people discussing things. Here are a few practical hints on this important part of the service.

a) The most important factor as far as I'm concerned is the length of the talk. This might sound a bit unspiritual, but the shorter the better. A news item on the TV or radio generally lasts only a few minutes. Even in fairly serious programmes the presentation chops and changes very quickly. This does not necessarily mean that they lack content or fail to deal with things seriously. On a news programme a great deal of information is conveyed in a very short time. We should not therefore be afraid to try to limit our talks to five minutes. The "thought for the day" type of talk on the radio does this very successfully. Once again this approach to preaching needs to go hand in hand with a systematic discipleship programme in small groups. A book I sometimes quote from is called *It's a Sin to Bore a Kid*. It may sound sacrilegious, but if you think about it what could be worse than boring someone with the Good News about Jesus? Our preaching needs to take this fact very seriously and we need to limit the length of our sermons in the light of the knowledge that most people's concentration time is about three minutes! (See the end of this chapter for a typical sermon outline.)

b) Who preaches is almost as important as what is said. If someone gets up to preach who is not respected by the group, whatever is said will be undermined by that fact. If the person speaking is known to be intolerant or lacking in concern for others, the message will lack credibility with the young people. The lifestyle of the preacher is very important. On the other hand if the person talking about God is known to be living the faith, that person will be respected. This doesn't mean that we have to be perfect to preach, far from it! In fact if the struggles and weaknesses of the preacher are there for everyone to see this will lead to them being respected. People listen to someone with whom they can identify. This means that it is good for the preacher to be a bit vulnerable about their own walk with God. It is also a good idea for the preaching to be done by someone from within the group itself. This makes for greater identification between the preacher and those listening and there is also more likelihood that what is said can be checked out in the preacher's life and seen to be true.

c) Speakers don't need to be experts. In fact we have a policy of using as many first time people as possible in the role of preacher. In this way young people can all get to have a say if they want to. It also means that they can talk about living the Christian life as it is. Their experience of being a teenager and struggling to live as a Christian gives their words a power and a genuineness which communicate however stumbling and hesitant the delivery. But there is a need for people to be encouraged to develop some basic skills. We meet with young people who are going to speak a couple of times before the service to help them plan what they are going to say and to give them some hints about delivery. We try to make sure that they don't read sermons from a piece of paper. This doesn't mean that they can't have notes, but there is a tendency to look at the notes rather than at the people you are talking to. We also give the preacher a few minutes to practise with the microphone just before the service. A quick run through also gives the group running the service a chance to encourage the preacher.

d) Using different people up front means that we do not foster a personality cult. For those of us working with young people tend to develop an unhealthy enjoyment at being the hero and being seen to be doing the right thing. Using young people to preach gets round this problem.

e) People like to listen to stories. We encourage story-telling as much as possible in our sermon time. In doing this, of course, we are following Jesus's example, but it's also true that everyone likes stories. What is a good movie, or a good soap opera, but just a story? We need to take a hint from the TV here and try to convey the Christian message in a story form. Stories are good, not just because they get people interested, but because they often touch us deeply at a number of different levels. We respond not just with our intellect but also with our emotions. For this reason it is really worthwhile to use stories as much as possible in preaching.

f) It is possible to make the whole of the sermon one long story. Re-telling Bible stories in this way can be a very creative way of getting into the Bible passage. To do it well you need to exercise your imagination and start to feel what it was like to live in a certain time and go through certain experiences. A book that does this well is *Imagining the Gospels* by Kathy Galloway, published by SPCK, which also gives good examples of the use of stories in church.

g) Stories are also important if they come from real life situations. When young people preach I encourage them to start a story from their own experience. Then what they say is more likely to make sense to everyone else, and they will be starting in the place where the rubber hits the road, that is, living out the Christian life in their everyday environment.

h) Real life experiences are very powerful and they need to be at the heart of our preaching. Alternative worship must be real and down-to-earth in the way it talks about the Christian Faith. A simple way of getting to everyday experiences very quickly in a sermon is to interview people about their experience of Jesus. This gives a chance for young people who don't want to preach to get up there and talk about their faith with a friendly presence there to prompt them. It is a good idea to talk the interview through beforehand so that they come prepared, though the odd unforseen question adds a bit of spontaneity. The main thing is to make sure that what you ask does not embarrass them or make them so uncomfortable that they clam up. The opposite problem is where you ask a question and the person simply ignores you and talks to the congregation as if you weren't there. One way to avoid this is to use a hand-held microphone and keep hold of it yourself. That way if they don't shut up you can just take the mike away and interrupt them!

i) One way to vary the sermon or interview is to use a panel of people to talk about an issue. This can work very well as long as it doesn't go on too long and if the people have some interesting things to say. One way to keep it lively is to use this approach for more personal or moral issues about which there is some debate and to make sure that the panel represents a variety of views. Of course you don't want too much of an argument because that may defeat the whole object of the exercise. But this approach does highlight the fact that interpreting the Bible needs to be a group activity that everyone should be involved with.

j) Taking this a stage further could involve getting all those who come to the service to read a passage, think about it, and comment on what they have learned from it. They could then write their ideas on a graffiti board. Another way to involve the congregation in the creation of the sermon is for one person to speak for a minute or so and then allow others in the congregation to add what they have been thinking. It is important to make sure that an argument or discussion does not take place. But if the rules are laid out fairly clearly at the beginning, e.g. that only one person speaks when holding the microphone and that we don't argue with someone else's ideas, then it should work. A potential problem, of course, is that people may be slow to speak and a horrible silence sets in. One way to avoid this is to have a few stooges around the room who are primed to get the ball rolling.

k) Finally here is a brief outline which I try to follow whenever I have to preach at a worship service. It is not, of course, a cast-iron, failsafe formula, but it contains guidelines which I find helpful.

- **Introduction:** Smile at the congregation and say something to warm them up a bit. Then introduce what the sermon is about, making sure that it is linked to a real issue or event in the lives of the young people. The best way to do this is by telling a story.
- **Bible story:** Re-tell a short story from the Bible in a lively but sensitive manner. Don't be afraid to fill in a few details and crack a few jokes, but be sure to get the point over clearly.
- **So what:** Say in a simple way why the Bible story sheds light on the situation that you have talked about. Make one point or if you must two. Give some idea about what action is expected as a result of what you have said.
- **Response:** Suggest a way that an aspect of the service, e.g. taking Communion, could be used as an act of commitment to action.
- **End:** Get off quick, don't hang around. Actually ending a talk is hard so I normally have a period of silence or a time when I pray. But the most important thing is to stop early and leave them wanting more!

11 · Prayer

Prayer should have a vital place in your plans for a service. But it would be a mistake to limit thinking about prayer to one particular slot in the worship. It has a much bigger part to play. In fact, prayer should be seen as part of the whole flow of the worship from the beginning to the end of the service (and indeed beyond it!).

Worship: a journey in prayer

Many of the classic books about prayer divide the subject up under headings: adoration, confession, petition, praise and thanksgiving[1]. These different aspects of prayer will nearly always form a vital part of the mix in a worship service. Praise may well be sung or danced, confession may be said aloud all together or silently, adoration may arise from the Bible reading or from the group looking at a particularly moving picture, but whatever form they take, many of the parts of the service could rightly be called prayer.

The service can be pictured as a journey which the whole congregation goes on together. This journey is an adventure in prayer. On this journey prayer is not static or even a passive pastime, but a way of reacting to a service which is very much alive. It demands that we get involved, that we risk a great deal of ourselves as we respond to everything that is going on in the service. Prayer is a risk because we are approaching a Holy God, a dangerous and unpredictable God, a God who will challenge our securities and our safety. It is for this reason that Anthony Bloom talks about prayer as a "dread adventure"[2]. Real prayer is scary!

In planning worship with young people we need to take seriously the fact that we will be setting out on an encounter with God. This sort of encounter will never be a superficial thing, it will always be mysterious and beyond our control. It is only the attitude of prayer which makes the difference between merely singing a song and entering genuinely into a time of worship and praise. Prayer sums up this kind of "entering in".

Thinking about worship in this way means the service must be carefully planned to allow the praying congregation to move from one prayerful response to another. For example there is a natural movement from confession and absolution where we are told that our sins are forgiven, to a time of praise where we can thank God for his forgiveness. In this way the whole service develops a sense of direction and flow. One way to make sure that this sort of flow happens is to think about what types of prayer we are expecting to explore in each part of the service. Here is an example of a simple service with the types of prayer added to the programme.

1. *First song:* Adoration
2. *Bible reading and talk:* Adoration/Confession
3. *Confession and absolution:* Confession
4. *Second song:* Thanksgiving and Praise
5. *The Peace:* Thanksgiving
6. *The Communion:* Praise and Adoration
7. *Prayers:* Petition
8. *Final song:* Thanksgiving

Planning the prayers

Even when we think about the whole of a service in terms of prayer, most services will still need a specific "prayer slot". A prayer time is important because it makes our response to God much more personal by focusing our attention. It can also be the best time to make specific requests to God. Once again there is a need to be as creative with this aspect of the service as possible. Here are a few ideas.

1. *Candles*

Candles are extremely useful when it comes to prayer. We use them regularly when we get together because they immediately create a prayerful atmosphere. The small fragile candlelight in a darkened room is a symbol of the faith we all share. There is a symbolic power in the lighting of a candle, which does help people to pray. One candle on its own in the middle of the group can be very effective. It focuses people's eyes towards it and then beyond it as the prayer deepens towards the source of all light. We have also used a great number of candles. One simple but powerful idea is to place about fifty small nightlights all together on the floor. Another is to give everyone a hand-held taper. These can be lit one from another to show how we share our faith with each other. Jesus blesses us as we meet in fellowship through every member of the group. Once again there is much to explore in the symbolism of candles (see Chapter 10).

2. *Music*

We often use music during our prayer times, usually as a backing track. On a few occasions, however, we have used music as an accompaniment to a time of silent meditation. This works extremely well, especially when a few words of introduction are said to help people to focus their thoughts on God.

These times of quiet may be the first time that some young people have had the space to sit still. Our lives tend to be very noisy and a few moments of quietness can be a very rare event. But some find silence very threatening and maybe a bit scary, so it is a good idea to introduce this sort of unstructured prayer gently and slowly. I usually ask the group to close their eyes and invite God to come to them, perhaps suggesting that they tell God about something which is on their minds. Young people need to be reassured that it is okay for your mind to wander a bit. The main thing, I tell them, is to be open to God touching you in his way. There's no need to force things, just try to sit and wait for God to make himself known. Of course this can be extremely threatening and using music to cover the natural embarrassment of sitting in silence is very helpful. Music can be a comforting thing when you start to pray for the first time since it relaxes you and also creates a safe and familiar environment. Young people are used to listening to records and tapes, but music is also able to move us beyond ourselves. It creates a space where God's Spirit can be at work.

It is a good idea to lead silent prayers without music once in a while just to vary the menu a bit. But silent prayer is best used with groups that already have some experience of praying.

3. *Using a set phrase to pray*

Leaving people to be open to God may be a bit challenging for some groups. My own experience of silent prayer as a young person was that time seemed to stand still. I felt anxious sitting in a room with a whole load of people who didn't say anything! One way to help a group with this is to give them a short phrase which can help them as they pray. "Lord have mercy" is a good one, or a part of the Lord's prayer such as "Forgive us our sins" or "Thy Kingdom come". The main thing is to make sure that the phrase is big enough to allow people to explore lots of different thoughts and responses as they say it. It should produce a simple but profound framework around which people can put their own particular concerns or situations.

One prayer I have found to be very helpful is the Jesus Prayer: "Lord Jesus Son of God have mercy on me a sinner". This short prayer can be used with a very simple breathing exercise. When you breathe in you say the "Lord Jesus" bit, and when you breathe out you say the "Have mercy on me" bit. This way of praying involves the body as well as the mind and is a very simple form of meditation that most people can enjoy[3]. This sort of breathing exercise is also a way to stay focused in prayer.

4. *Using pictures*
We often use pictures in our prayer times. One way is simply to project onto the screens images that remind you of the holiness of God. Icons are pretty good for this, or you could use a picture of Christ on the cross or a news photograph of a current event. These pictures help in creating the atmosphere for prayer, and they can also be very good used as a guide to the prayers. For example, if you are asking God to be at work in the world it can be helpful to use pictures of the homeless or of war or of people suffering. You can say prayers from the front as you look at the pictures, or you can get everyone to pray out loud as they look at the pictures, or you can let people say their own prayers silently as they look at them.

Whatever way they are used, it must be said that it takes a little time for groups to get into using pictures in this way. I personally find it quite hard to pray when I have my eyes open and so I find that I have to look at the pictures and then close my eyes to pray, holding the picture in my mind as I do it. It is a good idea therefore to give some guidance to the group as to how they can use the picture in their own prayer.

5. *Praying together*
To be prayed for by other people is one of the most powerful things that I have experienced. For young people involved in worship the experience of hearing someone else pray for them is often both moving and affirming. It builds them up, especially when this is something which they are encouraged to do for each other. We try to model this approach to prayer for all young Christians because it is such a source of spiritual renewal and growth. In the first instance we use this form of

prayer silently in our small groups. One way to do this is to ask people to look at the people next to them on their left and on their right and then to pray for that person. If they want they can put their hands on the shoulder of the person they are praying for. After a few minutes you pray for the person on the other side. Praying silently in this way can be very powerful, but we also encourage people to pray out loud. We do this before every service, both behind the scenes and up front, especially for those taking a leading role.

6. *Praying out loud*
Speaking out loud in a group can be very hard for a young person. One way to make it comfortable and non-threatening is to sit in a circle and invite people to pray around the circle one after the other. After each person has prayed they tell the next person that they have finished by touching them gently on the arm. If you make it clear that it's okay if you don't pray out loud then people don't feel under any pressure to perform. You also avoid any embarrassing silences. The good thing about this way of organizing prayer is that it creates a safe place for young people to choose to pray out loud if they want to without making the whole thing too open-ended and risky.

7. *Praying up front*
Leading the prayers in a service can be very exciting for young people. We often get two or three young people to work together on the prayers so that they can help each other think it through. Working in this way can be an important learning process for them, as well as a stretching experience as they put down on paper what they want to say to God. They also learn a lot from each other by working in a group on this part of the service. On the whole we prefer to do the prayers in this way because it involves a larger number of people in the up front part of the service. But if it is to work well, people who are new to this role need the opportunity to get used to using the microphone. The main reason for this is that most

of us tend to talk quietly when we pray! But we also need to be aware of the pace of the prayers. If you go too fast it loses its power, but if you go too slow it can be a bit dull!

8. *Using set prayers*
The rich store of prayers which the Church has used over the centuries, including the Lord's Prayer, are not often used with young people. I feel we need to introduce them into our worship as much as possible because they are a rich part of the Church's tradition. The Lord's Prayer is simply packed with meaning and it can bear a good deal of use! Other prayers which are perhaps less well known can also spice up the mix from time to time. A good source of these is, believe it or not, the Anglican Prayer Book!

The Bible is also full of short prayers which have been a part of many people's prayer lives. "The Grace" is a good one of these, and it can be used in a variety of ways. One way is to get everyone to hold hands as they say it. Of course this can be a bit corny, but I'm always struck by how powerful the simple action of joining hands in a circle can be.

9. *Singing prayers*
Songs are a really good way to help people to pray. We often start singing a song and then let the music fall away until it is a very quiet melody in the background. Then over the top of this people can be invited to pray silently. This works well in our Communion service where we sing "Lamb of God who takes away the sins of the world". After singing it a few times we lead the simple confession which we flash up on one of the screens for everyone to say out loud, then after some silent prayer and the absolution we pick the song up again and sing it through a few times.

Another way to use songs in our prayers is to sing a simple chorus a few times to get people into it and then leave a large gap for some short intercessions to be said over the top of the music. At the end of each intercession we sing the chorus. One of the songs we use like this has the short chorus "Father be with us, hear us, heal us".

Songs can also be used quietly as a form of prayer in themselves. People can be invited to kneel or sit and then sing the song to God. The best form of song to use in this way is one which is very short which can be repeated over and over. Taizé songs are good, though a bit old-fashioned in their style of music, and singing in Latin can be a bit of a turn-off. We've found, however, that a simple one-line song works well in alternative worship.

10. *Writing down prayers*

A good way to vary the prayer life of a group is to get people to write prayers down. We've used this method of praying in a variety of different ways. One idea that worked well is to get everyone to write down a prayer and then put it in a hat. Then one by one the prayers are read out either by everyone taking it in turns or by one person. Of course this only works if people write clearly! Another way is to get people to write down prayers and then as a symbolic gesture place them in front of a cross or a picture of Jesus. When we did this as a confession we once took the pile of sins written on the pieces of paper outside and burned them!

Prayers can also be drawn. We have used pictures as a form of prayer in lots of different ways. A simple approach is to get everyone to draw their prayer and then pin them on large boards, then when music is playing, people can go and look at the pictures and use them as a form of prayer. Another way of doing this is to get people to work together on simple collages, either by drawing, or by cutting up magazines and sticking pictures and words on a large sheet of paper. Once again these can be used as a guide for prayer by giving over a good space of time for people to look and pray with all of the different pictures. One more way is simply to invite people to pin their written prayers on a board and leave them there as a sign of their request being before God.

NOTES

1. See Anthony Bloom, *Living Prayer*; O. Hallesby, *Prayer*; Michael Hollings, *Day by Day*.
2. Bloom, *Living Prayer*, p9.
3. See Per-Olaf Sjogren, *The Jesus Prayer*.

12 · Sacraments and Symbols

Symbols are a part of our everyday lives. We all know that a red triangle on a road sign means that we have to beware of something, or that when red is showing on the traffic light we must stop. Young people also regularly use symbols in the way they create their sense of group identity. Wearing a particular pair of Nike baseball boots, for instance, immediately places you in a different group from the person who wears a pair of Dr Martens.

Christian worship is also highly symbolic. The most common symbol is the bread and wine used in the Communion, and water is used in Baptism. But symbolic actions, gestures, and words are so central to whatever we do when we worship that we sometimes fail to realize that they are in fact symbols. We may kneel or bow our heads to pray or sing songs about Jesus the Lamb, stand up when the minister walks into church, or simply shake hands with people during the service without thinking too much about the symbolic meaning behind these things[1].

The use of symbols in our worship has become a natural part of our behaviour. They are a part of our shared church culture. When young people start to experiment with new forms of worship they will also need to use symbols. Some they will bring from their own culture, for example the sight of a DJ standing behind a pair of record decks in a worship service is symbolic of a rave. Other symbols will be ones already used by the Church which have been adapted to suit the culture of the young people, e.g. receiving the bread and the wine in a Communion service while listening to a rock band playing.

A Christian approach to symbols

Symbols used in worship may come from youth culture or from the culture of the Church but the crucial factor is that the symbols we use speak of Christ. In fact a Christian approach to symbols will always start with the idea of Jesus himself being the true sign or symbol of God's activity in the world.

The Good News of the New Testament is about God becoming flesh and blood: a man called Jesus. As John says, "The word became a human being and, full of grace and truth, lived among us. We saw his glory, the glory which he received as the Father's only Son" (John 1:14). In John's gospel Jesus and the things he did are talked about as signs of God's presence among us. This fact is crucially important when we are talking about the way we use symbols in our worship. Jesus is the most important sign or symbol of God's presence and activity in the world. The fact that God used the everyday life of a human being to speak to us is very important because it shows how seriously he takes our humanity and our need to experience his spiritual presence through physical symbols. St Athanasius writing in the third century put it like this:

> Men had turned from the contemplation of God above, and were looking for Him in the opposite direction, down among created things and things of sense. The Saviour of us all, the Word of God in His great love took to Himself a body and moved as Man among men, meeting their senses, so to speak, half way. He became Himself an object for the senses, so that those who were seeking the Father through sensible things might apprehend the Father through the works which He, the Word of God, did in the body.[2]

St Athanasius puts his finger on the key issue here. God meets us in ways that we can understand and this means the world of physical signs and symbols. But Jesus when he left his disciples realized that they would need a continuing sign of his presence with them and, so at the Last Supper, he showed them how he wanted to be remembered in the breaking of bread and in the cup of wine.

Sacraments

The Christian Church recognizes that some symbols used in worship are special. Jesus gave us the Lord's Supper and invited us to continue to remember his death by repeating the actions of eating bread and drinking wine. Baptism and marriage are similarly endorsed in the gospels when Jesus takes part in them. To call these symbols sacraments is one way to remind ourselves continually that they are special. But these sacraments are also a place where God promises to meet us. Other symbols may be used by the Spirit to inspire us, but the sacraments are unique because God promises to be with us when we take part in them.

Christians we know are divided over the meaning of the sacraments. We disagree about Baptism and we are disunited in the interpretation of the Communion. It's not my intention to presume to try and sort out these difficulties here. People need to solve this one within their own church setting and tradition. But I do want to make a strong plea for alternative worship to take seriously the use of the sacraments.

It's been our experience that regular Communion with a group of young people has been a constant source of strength and encouragement. In a sense it takes you into another dimension of Christian experience. It is not just the fact the Communion service connects us to every other Christian community, it also unites us with one another in a symbolic way. We seem to get close to each other when we take Communion. But Communion is also at the same time a way to meet God in a very personal and deep way. Why this is so is a question for theological discussion. I simply want to say that Christian worship for young people which neglects this area will inevitably be ignoring a precious and spiritually enriching resource. Indeed Communion and baptism were gifts given us by Christ to help us grow in the Faith. So we should not be surprised when young people find them to be helpful in their lives – that is precisely what they were meant to be.

St Mary and John where JOY takes place is in the High Church tradition of the Church of England. We have wanted to include the sacraments in our worship as a sign of our unity with the Church. This meant having to agree to the regular discipline of confirmation and baptism for people who want to take Communion.

In the early days of JOY some young people who had not been confirmed did not take Communion. They went up to the priest during the service and he gave them a blessing. When I talked to them about this they told me they wanted to wait until they felt ready to enter into this aspect of the worship fully. The fact that they then had to go through a preparation for confirmation was a very enriching time for many of us. We used our fellowship groups as a time of learning for everyone in JOY. Then on the Saturday before Easter people from JOY joined with the regular congregation of St Mary and John at a joint service of baptism, confirmation and renewal of baptism vows. To join with the church in this way was an act of unity which also endorsed the view that membership of JOY was serious and a definite act of commitment. It encouraged the young people to see their attendance at the service as a long-term matter. As JOY grows we plan to repeat this process for new members every year.

Using a variety of symbols

The Communion is rightly central to Christian worship but we also use a great many other symbols. We believe in a God who is the creator. Everything we see or touch has been created by God and it continues therefore to bear his imprint. In the created world we are continually reminded of God the creator and Jesus through whom all things came into being. This is not only true of what we call "nature", it is also true of everything which we as humans create. Of course, we are fallen creatures and subject to sin and this will affect the things we create. Yet our ability to make things in itself reflects the image of God in our own make-up. This means that there are immense possibilities for the use of created things both human and "natural" as symbols in worship. Here are a few of the ideas we have developed in our own worship.

1. *Washing*

Christians have used water as a symbol of cleansing from the very beginning of the Church's history. Washing as a ritual act can be very powerful. One way to do this is to get people to wash each other's feet. This seemed a bit too difficult to organize, and taking off your shoes can be a very mixed experience!

A variation on the feet theme is to get people to wash their hands, symbolizing coming to God clean, washed of your sins. We used this action in one of our services where people were encouraged to wash their hands before they shared the Peace with each other. A couple of people held bowls of water and two more held towels. The congregation lined up in front of each of the bowls waiting their turn to wash their hands. The way this worked meant that you were standing in a queue waiting to wash your hands while the people a bit further on were already hugging each other and sharing the Peace of God. When your time came to wash your hands and join the joyful throng greeting one another, you were suddenly released into a new sense of community by the act of being symbolically made clean. The people holding the bowls and the towels symbolized how God uses the loving service and care of other people in the Body of Christ to make us whole.[3]

2. *Water*

In some traditions of the Church, water that has been blessed is used as a symbol of the purifying presence of God. We used this during one of our services to bring a new dimension to our prayer. Sprinkling the water around can be a bit distracting during a prayer time! A better way is to encourage people to dip their finger in it and make the sign of the cross on their forehead. Water that has been blessed is also used in baptism, so making the sign of the cross on your forehead can be a reminder of God's promise to us in baptism and a further act of commitment.

3. *Shaking hands*

In the Anglican Communion Service there is a place where people are encouraged to shake hands and greet each other, called the Peace. This part of the service is always very popular in JOY. Young people are very "touchy-feely". They like to hug each other, kiss each other, or at least the ones I know do!

Making the most of this part of the service can be very helpful. We generally mill around for a good ten minutes or so and it seems to go better if we play an up-beat dance track while it's going on. With groups new to the service we make sure that we explain what's going on. After a short introduction a bit of holy chaos can break out as people start to greet each other and chat. This is really important because it allows for a time of warmth and human contact as well as a large measure of informality, always a hit with young people if it is in good measure and well defined within the whole pattern of the service. Sharing God's peace in this way means that everyone can experience what it means to be a part of God's blessing to everyone else. The Peace is therefore a very sacred act as well as being good fun.

On a practical note, it is sometimes difficult to get the service back on track if everyone is chatting and wandering around. To avoid yelling at people to sit down and shut up we generally end the Peace with a song which pulls the group back together and focuses them on the next part of the service. We don't announce this song, we just start it and people seem to get back into shape, and they can start singing when they are ready.

4. *Candles*

Light and darkness are extremely powerful symbols and so we use them as much as possible. Because we worship later in the evening it is nearly always dark. We never use the church's lighting because it is quite bright and feels very impersonal. Candlelight in a darkened church seems to create an immediate atmosphere of prayer and worship. But we also use candles to symbolize where the "action" is in the service, which is generally the altar and wherever the reading, prayers and sermon take place.

Candles are used as a symbol of the Lord's presence in our worship. The act of lighting them becomes a symbolic gesture which speaks of God's Spirit entering the worship. Sometimes we start the service with people lighting candles which are placed in a circle in the centre of the worship area. Lighting the candles showed that something special was going to happen. God was going to be with us.

Candles are also a symbol of our prayer. In one service we encouraged people to light a candle to signify their prayer for a friend or a relative who had been in their minds during the prayer time.

Finally we have used hand-held candles as a way to symbolize the light of Christ in each of our lives. This works best if the whole church is in darkness and we light each others' candles from a central candle, so that the light slowly spreads just as the light of Jesus spreads from one person to another.

5. *Incense*

Some people may feel uneasy about the use of incense. My own parents connected it with drugs. But throughout its history the Christian Church has used incense as a symbol of the presence of the Spirit in our midst. In our own service we have used it from time to time and it does seem to bring a new sense into our worship, as well as creating pretty patterns in the lights! One tip is to get hold of something to waft it around with, otherwise you end up using a lot of the stuff and it can be very expensive! We avoid using joss sticks because of their connections with Eastern religion and we stick to good old-fashioned church incense.

6. *Circles*

For a number of different reasons circles and circle dances are very much in vogue at the moment. (Chapter 14 deals with dance in more detail.) Many Christian feminists have experimented with different ways of using this sort of activity in worship. At the most simple level, sitting in a circle can speak very powerfully of the fact that we are all equal in the sight of God. This is especially powerful if those leading the service also sit in the circle. If you think about it, the fact that leaders sit on seats raised above everyone at the front with the whole congregation looking at them symbolizes a particular view of church leadership. This may not be what we want in a new kind of worship where young people are involved in creating the worship. This idea can be created quite simply by sitting in a circle. We also use circles to share the Peace with each other. A simple way to do this is to get people to stand in a circle and then turn alternately left and right. They then greet the person they are facing and move on to the next person, slowly progressing around the circle and greeting people as they go.

7. *Pictures*

Chapter 15 will deal with aspect of worship in greater depth, but it is worth noting at this point that pictures can be powerful symbols of God's presence. Pictures are also a good way to symbolize young people's lives and culture as a part of worship. Using slide projectors an image can be flashed on a screen and used to direct people's prayer and worship. Images such as a Coke bottle, a pop star, an icon, a picture of a landscape, in fact almost anything can become part of the symbolic language of worship if it is used sensitively within the framework and flow of the service.

8. *The Cross*

Christian people have adopted the cross as their own symbol, but young people have also from time to time used this symbol in their own way. A silver cross can often be seen round a young person's neck or hanging from an earring, while hippies used to wear large wooden crosses on a piece of rope round their neck. It makes sense, then, to use the cross in our worship. A cross projected on a screen could simply be part of the architecture of the worship space. But it is easy to make a cross yourself and this can involve young people in creating a part of the worship, especially if they have some practical skills.

There are times when the cross can be more integral to the worship. Taking your cares or sins to the foot of the cross has been a consistent and rich image in Christian worship. Sometimes we get people to write their concerns on a piece of paper and then place it at the foot of the cross. This is a very simple and powerful way of using the cross in worship. In some churches they encourage people to approach a picture of Christ on the cross, and pray, or kiss the cross, or light a candle in front of it. This may not be up your street but all of these ideas can be helpful in getting people physically involved in the worship. Of course, by doing this we are not seeking to convey the idea that the cross has any automatic or magical power, it is simply a symbol of the death of Christ.

9. *People*

People are one of the most powerful symbols of all. When a young person looks round during a service he or she will be taking in everyone who is there and forming judgements. It's a daunting thought that we are indeed symbols of God's presence to each other. Worship has a human side to it as well as a divine aspect, and we should not underestimate the effect on a young person of other young people worshipping. The fact that people are symbols in worship also has an effect on who we choose to lead up front. In our services we try as much as possible to mix the ages, sex, class and race of the people who lead parts of the service, to show that everyone can have a part in our worship.

We also try to strike a balance between informality and formality. For instance, our services are led by young people who dress however they want to, while the priest always wears all his ceremonial gear just as he would in church on Sunday morning. He doesn't do this for some legal church reason. We have actually chosen that he dresses in his robes because of the symbolic references of his role among us. By wearing his robes he is saying clearly that our service is just as valid as any other, and is also making clear that he is present as a servant of the young people in preparing the bread and the wine for Communion.

NOTES

1. For more on symbols in Christian worship see "Sign, Symbol" in *A New Dictionary of Liturgy and Worship*, ed. J.G. Davies.
2. St Athanasius, *On the Incarnation*, p43.
3. I'm grateful to Sam Adams for this insight.

13 · Music

Music is close to young people's hearts. In fact it has often been the most important factor in the creation of different youth sub-cultures. But music has also played a very central role in Christian worship and many of the new movements which have renewed the Church down the ages have placed a great emphasis on music.

The Salvation Army is a good example here. William Booth was interested in making his worship contemporary so he took popular music-hall tunes and wrote Christian lyrics to them. Today the musical scene is a great deal more complex than it was in the nineteenth century, but there is still a great deal of common ground between the work of William Booth and the new movement towards alternative forms of worship based on youth culture. We certainly share the conviction that Christian worship needs to have a very contemporary approach to music.

Keeping up-to-date

Most adults feel a sense of inadequacy when young people talk about music. For one thing popular music is always changing. There are new instruments, new technologies which make different sounds, and every week on TV, there are new "stars" who seem to emerge from nowhere. Just keeping up with the pop scene is a full-time job. But even if you did manage to keep up the chances are that you would still be out of touch with the taste of many groups of young people in your local area.

The problem is that young people develop complex relationships with a great many different styles of music. I remember when I was a Christian rock musician travelling around the country, I was truly baffled at the different responses of young people to the sort of music that I played. Many was the time when I went down a storm in one school, only to find that when I was at the next school in the same area I was a total flop! When I talked to the young people after the concerts I started to realize that the success of the gig did not depend on how well I was playing, it was purely to do with what kind of music was acceptable in each of the schools. In the one school my music was fairly close to what they liked, in the next school I was quite simply out of touch.

I can't stress too much how difficult it is for adults to try to predict what kinds of music will appeal to young people. This fact, quite apart from any other, should lead us to make sure that as we develop new forms of worship we do so in partnership with the young people themselves. It is only by talking with our own particular group and by listening to their tapes and CDs that we will have any idea of their style of music. This sort of relationship is essential if our worship is ever to have the right sort of musical impact.

Live worship

Singing songs and choruses is at present very important to Christian worship, so important that it is hard to conceive of worship which does not have an element of singing in it. The problem is that young people are often very unwilling to sing. Actually this is not entirely true. Just think of the crowd at a football match, or the way people sing along with the songs of a well-known band at a big concert. Karaoke is another popular phenomenon. But all of this seems a long way away from the sort of music and singing that we do week by week in church.

One tempting solution would be to decide that singing need not be part of alternative worship. Imagine, no more embarrassing situations where a song goes down like a lead balloon! But singing can have a significant place in worship with young people. In the first place singing in a group creates a feeling of unity. People bond together as they sing a song. But singing is also important because it uniquely opens us to the Spirit of God. There is something very intimate and personal about our voice. It is our very own instrument, and when we sing we use our own bodies to make music. The voice in song is a genuinely personal expression of worship. It is for this reason that the Spirit uses singing so regularly to bless us. It would be crazy therefore to abandon singing without working at it with a group of young people.

The best way that I have found to use music in worship is to get young people involved in writing and performing it. If they are given the time and space to write the worship material themselves, there is a real chance that not only will its style suit your group, there is also a strong chance that the singing side of things will work out as well! Writing all of your own songs can be tough, and they can be supplemented by songs which other people have written. Some of the existing church songs have been very popular in our worship, but the new type of chorus tends to be less successful than old chestnuts like "Standing in the need of Prayer" and the hymn "Father, hear the prayer we offer".

DJ praise

Music used for worship does not have to be "live". There are a great many occasions where recorded music is much more useful. With a pair of decks and a P.A. it is possible to add spice by playing the right sort of records at the right points in the service. Dance tracks can be very good as the warm-up to a service, while during the prayers or Communion we play more restrained music. Needless to say preparation and skill are needed as well as a sensitivity to the way the music is affecting the feel of the worship.

JOY has occasionally held DJ workshops to help young

people develop the skills needed to work the record decks. DJs at raves are extremely creative in the way they operate the disco decks, not only talking over the music but also fading records in and out to create a new mix.

Hiring or buying disco gear may be financially beyond some groups, but you can get roughly the same effect by using a couple of tape recorders linked to a hi-fi system. The main drawback is that it can be difficult to cue the tape in exactly the right place. With normal disco gear you can cue records up a lot easier. But you can get round this with a pair of headphones. One tip is to use as many tapes as you can. One song per tape is ideal because then you can start all of them at exactly the right point.

What sort of music the DJ plays will depend entirely on the sort of worship service that is being planned and the culture of the young people who come. Christians are a bit sensitive about popular music and there are many different views on whether we should listen to this or that sort of music. When it comes to what music we use in worship, these sensitivities are increased by about 1 million! People get offended very easily because what goes on in church means so much to them. In planning alternative worship there will always be problems around the issue of what sorts of music are appropriate for use in church. This chapter is not a guide through these problems, but I personally always ask myself two important questions.

1. What does the piece of music mean to the young people involved in the worship? It may well be that the average churchgoer thinks it an incitement to riot and murder, but the young people may react to the same piece of music quite differently. To my mind the older people need to learn about the music from the younger ones and if their learning process involves a bit of hot steam now and then, that's okay by me.

2. Does the music, as it is understood by the young people involved, add anything to the worship? If it does not

contribute anything to the flow of the service then it's not worth getting upset over it.

I don't see much problem with using all sorts of music in alternative worship, including some classical or ethnic folk music. After all, if Pavarotti is good enough for football, why not use some of his religious stuff in church? TV adverts aimed at young people use all sorts of different types of music. In worship the main thing is to let young people have a good deal of say in what is being used. But at the end of the day you will only really know if something works by trying it out.

Some people may be wary of using "non-Christian" music in a worship service. I don't feel that we need to restrict ourselves to Christian music, but some care needs to be exercised. The most important factor is how the young people involved in the worship experience that particular track rather than whether the artists were Christian or not. In the last resort if people are led to worship by what they hear then that is what matters most. Obviously a record which advocated something which went against Christian worship, e.g. singing Hari Krishna, is to be avoided. But often ideas expressed in dance records are spiritual without being very specific about what they mean. Lyrics such as "Love is the message" or "Your love is lifting me" could mean a variety of things. It is perfectly legitimate to use songs like this in Christian worship because the meaning of the lyric is in the heads of the people dancing, not in the intentions of the person who made the record (whatever they may be). Our favourite dance track at the moment is by Soul to Soul, whose main lyric has a particular meaning for people involved in our worship service: "Joy is a new sensation, rocking the nation."

A word of warning here though. It's worth listening very carefully to a track before you use it in worship, especially a dance track, because they may hold some surprises. It's easy to listen to a small part of a song and miss the erotic noises at the end of the record because you haven't played it that far.

Next thing you know during a Communion service you have a few very unhelpful moments and a very embarrassed DJ!

Using music in worship

Here are a few ideas which might provide some pointers for the use of music in worship.

1. *Background music*

Recorded music is very useful as a backing to other elements in the service. The technique TV documentaries use to combine commentary with a backing track can be used throughout a service. It works for prayers and readings in particular because it helps us to concentrate. For this to work well it's usually best to use a piece of instrumental music rather than a song with lots of words, which could interfere with what is being said. One simple technique to punctuate a dynamic prayer time is to fade the music down while the person prays and then bring up the volume straight afterwards while people dwell on the prayers.

2. *Creating a smooth flow*

Recorded music, especially when it is used throughout a service, can create a good sense of direction and continuity. The recorded music must fade in and out of the service with slickness, e.g. at the end of a chorus the recorded background music should start to fade in immediately. This technique is very helpful because it can cover up the spaces where people leading the service are getting ready to do the next thing. If recorded music is used all the way through the service, it becomes the foundation which you return to every time the service moves from one highlight to the next.

It's also true that when you are used to music being there as a backing to the readings and the prayers, silence can be used much more creatively as a deliberate aid to worship. The absence of a backing track can create special emphasis in the service, for example when someone gives a talk or a sermon.

3. *Tapping into the roots*
The problem with so much Christian worship material is that it has its roots in middle-of-the-road folk music. For this reason we hardly ever use established "Christian music" in JOY. The music which most young people are listening to comes with a very different pedigree. Rock, rap and hip hop are essentially different animals to the kind of music currently used in church services. This fact, in itself, is very important when we come to work on new kinds of songs and choruses for alternative worship.

One problem which we need to overcome is the fact that these styles of music do not easily lend themselves to community singing. Getting a worship song right therefore takes some work. We have found, for instance, that melody lines need to be very simple and catchy. With rap music which is usually characterized by one person speaking it is particularly difficult to get people to join in, but a simple rhythmic pattern of words repeated enough times works successfully. There is also room for a simple chorus with a rapped verse performed by the artists. Dance music on the other hand is very flexible because it can have a number of different chants or choruses featured over the top of a basic beat. Once again, though, the bits where you are expected to sing need to be fairly predictable and regular otherwise people can't follow it very easily.

4. *Familiarity breeds worship*
Particular pieces of music can become more meaningful the more they are used. It is remarkable how a dance track used in prayer or meditation can evoke the same kinds of feelings of prayer when you hear it the next time. This fact in itself seems to me to be a good reason for using the same tracks again and again in worship. In this way you build up your own shared culture of worship and this in itself can be very helpful,

for too much variety can leave people a bit lost in a service. Of course you can over-do repetition and kill a song off if you are not careful. As with most things it's a question of balance.

5. *A word about copyright*

The good news about copyright is that no royalty is charged for the performance of music in a service of public worship. This means that you do not need the usual kind of licence from the Performing Rights Society (which handles copyright issues for all composers) if you are playing records in a service. However this does not extend to the reproduction of lyrics on handouts, slides or even on hand-written OHP slides. When you are using songs from a Christian song book the odds are that these songs are covered by the licence scheme set up by the major Christian music publishers[1]. For more details about this scheme contact Christian Copyright Licensing Ltd (CCLI), PO Box 1339, Eastbourne, E Sussex, BN21 4YF.

6. *Getting too technical*

One of the problems with using music throughout a worship service, especially if it is rock music or dance music, is that you can easily lose the human touch. Some of the songs we play in JOY use a good deal of modern synthesizers and drum machines. To overcome the problems of performing these live we generally record them on a small four-track tape recorder and then sing over the top of them. We have found that having the backing track on tape has some drawbacks because everything has to follow the exact sequence of the tape. It is very easy to get out of time with the tape and then you are in a real mess! We try therefore to vary the diet at JOY by sometimes using a live band or even just one acoustic guitar. Unlike a backing track live musicians can react to the way the worship is developing.

7. *Serving in worship*

Playing music in a worship service is not very easy. In the first place it is not like a gig where things can flow at their own pace. In a service, songs happen at predicted times and if you are caught with your guitar unplugged or your microphone turned off it can disturb the flow. Concentration and professionalism in performance are very important because the band has to become to some extent invisible so that people can concentrate on the worship. If attention is continually being drawn to the band because of mistakes or technical hitches then some of the feel of the worship is inevitably lost. The same holds true for the way the band performs the songs. All of this means that the members of the worship band need to know what they are doing. It can be hard for them to worship freely because they have always to be one step ahead of the action in the service. It is important that young people in the band see the music as their way of worshipping. They are serving everyone else by doing their bit in the service as best they can. But we try to make sure that the same people are not up front every week so that they can experience a service as a normal member of the congregation from time to time.

NOTE

1. For more on copyright see *Keep Music Legal* by Simon Law and Eric Lives.

14 · Dance

I get very embarrassed about dancing, but it hasn't always been that way. In fact there was a time when I would "freak out" to some rockin' number at the church youth club disco.

Looking back on that now I realize that as a teenager I found something very freeing about dancing in that way. I was expressing myself and that was all that mattered. I suppose I didn't look very pretty. Shaking your head up and down in time to the music does lack a certain grace, I now realize, and yet in those moments I did experience a sort of completeness. At the time music was one of the most important things in my life and as I danced I felt that I was being caught up in the experience of the music in a unique way. There was a joy about it which was very deep and seemed to come from inside and take me up to a new plane. I felt really alive. Maybe the reason for this was that when I was dancing I began to get in touch with my deepest feelings.

I remember one very painful time when I was given my marching orders by my current girlfriend at a disco. I wandered back into the church hall where the music was playing. I felt pretty bad and at first I was not really dancing, but as I began to get into it I started to dance my emotions out. After a while the songs they were playing seemed to sum up everything that I was going through and as I danced, my feelings welled up inside me. This sounds a bit self-indulgent, but at the time the fact that I could lose myself in the music was very helpful. After a while I started to feel a good deal better about what had gone on. Somehow by dancing out my feelings I had managed to come to terms with them.

Dancing days are here again

Dance as self-expression and as a means to wholeness has a lot to offer the Christian Church. Let's face it, most church services in Britain are very static. We don't seem to move around very much in church, let alone dance. Of course recently there has been a movement towards dance in church with the performance of a "sacred dance", though this is usually very limited in its movement, and as far as I'm concerned in its appeal as well! For some people it may be helpful, but it seems a long way from the sort of dance I was getting into at the disco and it certainly doesn't generate the same kind of emotional response in me.

Movement of another kind has started to come into worship at events like Spring Harvest. Here we see people jig about a bit as they worship in what has been called the "House Church hop". Once again it falls a long way short of what most young people get up to when they dance at parties or raves. For many Christians this sort of movement in worship can be very freeing and meaningful and it does point towards the use of our bodies in worship in new ways. One problem with this kind of dancing is that Christian choruses and worship songs are often not written with dance in mind. The rhythm is such that there is not much in the way of movement and dance that you can do when you sing them. This, I'm sure, is one of the reasons why people just hop from one foot to the other and raise their arms in the air when they worship in this way. To put it bluntly, that's all you can do when you are trying to follow the beat of this sort of chorus. When you also consider that we are often sitting or standing in rows because of the way the chairs are arranged, it's understandable why we are limited simply to a jig in our modern worship. But maybe there is another reason why we seem so limited in our use of dance in worship.

Letting go

The first time I went to a Christian rave I found the whole experience very challenging. The rave was organized by the group from St Aldate's who later formed part of JOY. As well as the normal flashing lights and loud music there were TVs silently showing pictures all around the room. In the front there was a massive picture of Jesus and all the people dancing seemed to face in that direction. Looking at these dancing people I realized that although they were dancing in much the same way as they would at a secular rave, they were in fact worshipping. Some of their movements were adapted from charismatic worship. They raised their hands up in the air with their palms facing upwards. Their faces showed expressions of ecstatic praise that I recognized from seeing the same sort of thing in church.

Seeing these people dancing and worshipping was a strange and threatening experience. As I've got older I've become very inhibited about dancing but there was more to it than just being a bit self-conscious. There was also a real reluctance on my part to enter into the experience of worshipping with my whole body in dance. In JOY we very often have times when people are encouraged to dance during the worship. Sometimes I find myself standing on the edge of things not quite ready to let go in worship to the extent that others do. Often I am reduced to a little jig myself precisely because I find the challenge of giving myself in worship very difficult.

It's at this point that I go back to my experiences of dancing as a young person. In the disco I was able to use dance as a means to express my inner self in a very profound way. I could even say that my dancing was a "sacred act" because it was integrating body, mind and spirit. In our worship times I feel a profound reluctance to dance because I realize that if I really start to let go it will make me extremely vulnerable. Dancing will open me to God's presence in ways that perhaps I will not be able to control. This I must admit scares me.

This has been a long confession, but I hope what I'm getting at has started to become clear. Dance can play a very important part in worship. Each of us is body, mind and spirit and one of the mystical things about the experience of dance, especially when it is free and expressive, is that as we begin to move we start to find a unity within ourselves. In worship this concept of being before God as whole beings waiting on his blessing and rejoicing in his presence is very powerful. But the deep truth here is that we only experience this unity when we are willing to let go.

Letting go in dance means that we have to start to "physically" worship. There are no two ways about it. How many times have you been at a party standing on the edge of things when someone who is dancing calls out your name and encourages you to join in? For those of us a bit hung up about dancing this kind of situation is very challenging. There is a choice here: will I join in or will I not? In the context of worship this kind of choice is even more challenging because dance is now about a willingness, or lack of willingness, to open up to God. To choose to dance is to be abandoned in your body, mind and spirit to God.

Thinking about dance in worship means that we take seriously the fact that we are feeling people, people who can move and be alive in the presence of God. It also means that we are open to God in a new and life-changing way because in dance things come to the surface.

You really move me

The saying that actions speak louder than words is most definitely true when it comes to dancing in a spirit of worship. I use the words "dancing in a spirit of worship" deliberately because not all dance will be Christian worship. We worship God when what we do, be it singing or dancing, is directed towards the glory of God. There needs to be a clear intention on our part to use what we are doing as a means of turning towards God in response to his love revealed in the life of Jesus.

It is not so much a question of how we move our bodies, it is more to do with what is going on inside us when we dance. We need to learn how to unite our bodies and our minds in this kind of worship. Worshipping through dance is at first quite strange but I can honestly say that if you stick with it, it becomes very rewarding.

Most young people will to some extent or another have dance as part of their youth culture. Presently with raves on the up and up (in more ways than one!) dance has become a very unifying feature in youth culture. To dance at a rave can be an exhilarating experience, involving a feeling of being deeply at one with everyone else and with yourself. But these feelings, though akin to Christian worship, are not the same thing. Young people will need to learn about worship and dance. It is important to make explicit the fact that to worship in dance involves opening yourself up to God. As we dance we are giving ourselves to him, and our movement is an expression of that self-giving. By dancing we are making a physical offering of ourselves to God. This kind of offering does not happen at a rave.

Christian worship is not just about a good feeling or a sense of togetherness. To worship means that the Spirit of God comes and moves among us, and it is this fact that makes it entirely different from a normal rave. Part of the mystery of Christian worship is the fact that when we give ourselves to God by singing or speaking, by keeping still and silent, or by dancing. God comes and meets us in that place. Worship is a two-way process. Our dance is a response to the love of God in Jesus, but as we dance we begin to experience the presence of God coming close to us by his Spirit. I like to think that as we dance the Spirit of God is there dancing with us touching each of us deeply as we open ourselves to his presence amongst us.

It is because of the fact that God's Spirit is there when we dance that worshipping in this way can be so powerful. As we move we do not just jig around, we are in a very deep way starting to express ourselves. This, of course, is exactly what God's Spirit finds attractive. As we dance we are in effect opening ourselves up to his touch. When we let go we can let God in.

Let's dance
Here are a few practical ideas on using dance in worship.

1. *Getting things going*
Dance is a good way to start a service, since there is no better way for people to start to get into the flow of things. But like any party or disco it usually takes a while for things to get going. Starting a service with dance can be a bit nerve-racking. People tend to take a while to defrost, they wander in and sit down for a while, it's as if they need to drink-in the atmosphere at first. It's only when there are a good few people there that they start to warm up and move about freely in the worship area.

One way to get things going quickly is to have a few of the regulars there dancing right from the start. DJs will have a few tricks up their sleeves to help people start to dance by choosing particular records, but worship will only break out as the congregation begins to unwind. This in itself is no bad thing because it reminds us that worship comes from the people and the Spirit of God, not from the records or the flashing lights. It's worth leaving a good deal of time for the atmosphere to warm up if you start a service in this way because you are dependent on the group feel of the congregation.

2. *Worshipping outside of a service*
Young people dance at parties, at gigs and at raves and it is possible for these to be times when they can also worship. A number of people who go to JOY make a habit of going to clubs to have a good time. This in their mind will also involve using the occasion to worship God. You don't have to be in church

to worship God by dancing, just like you don't have to be in church to pray. To worship at a party by dancing simply means that you start to direct your thoughts and your movements towards God. You consciously reach out to God and invite him to be there with you in that place. For some this is just a personal experience, but others in JOY talk of the way God has used their presence at the party or the rave to touch someone else.

In a way this sort of worship has an important symbolic power. By worshipping in the very place where other people are perhaps taking drugs or living out their own fantasies in an unhealthy way, turning to God and inviting his presence into the situation is to make an important statement that Jesus is in fact Lord of all. No place is too dark or too distant for the light of Christ to reach in and touch people, even at clubs and raves. Worshipping in dance in these places is one way to make this truth a reality.

3. *Keeping in touch*
Christians involved in alternative worship need to keep in touch with current youth culture. When worship is based on dance culture they need to be visiting clubs and raves if the creativity of the Christians is not going to end up being out of touch[1].

4. *Dangerous dance*
Some Christian young people look on dance as a destructive part of their old lives. They find dancing a problem even in church, because it is associated with things they want to turn their backs on. This in itself does not mean that dancing is bad, it's the way it was used in the past that was wrong. It is worth trying to be sensitive to this and leaving space in the worship time to explain what worshipping through dance is all about. Spending time talking about dance could kill the atmosphere so it needs to be handled well. One way would be to get some people who worship in this way to share freely what God has

done for them through dance. But the best way to teach people about dance in worship is for them to see other Christians using dance in this way.

5. *Performance dance*

There is a place for dance as a performance in worship. Much sacred dance may leave a lot to be desired, but modern dance can be a very vivid and moving form of communication. As with most things conflict, problems and violence look most dramatic in a dance created for other people to watch. One reason for this is that violent movements are easier to do well than peaceful gliding types of dance. In JOY we have used this type of dancing to speak about the pain and anger which many of us feel in our personal relationships. As with all aspects of worship, we should try to make sure that what happens has grown out of the life of the group. It is much better to get people to write their own dance and perform it because they will feel a sense of ownership of it.

6. *Atmosphere*

If people are going to dance in a free and uninhibited way, there needs to be the right atmosphere. This will depend on the mood of the congregation, but there are a few commonsense things which we can do to encourage people to dance. Darkness is very important. If you are going to let your hair down then you need to feel that you have some privacy and you are out of the public gaze. A suitable gloom is all you need – complete darkness would involve a few too many collisions! Music for dancing needs to have a good rhythm, but it also needs to be loud. A few flashing lights or other suitable illumination can help in building the right kind of atmosphere for dancing.

7. *Ending with dance*

The end of a service needs to be thought about carefully. One very effective idea we use frequently is to invite people to stay around and worship by dancing. One advantage of having this sort of "rave" at the end of the service is that it can progress at its own pace and people can hang around and chat without feeling too much pressure to dance if they don't want to. Finishing with dancing is also a really good way to let people respond in worship to the way God has touched them during the service. A rave time during the service breaks up the flow because it demands a different kind of discipline and works at a different pace. It is spontaneous and flowing, while the normal kind of service is more structured with different types of communication such as sermons or readings which fit less easily into a dance setting. This does not mean that a service may not be orientated towards dance, but it restricts the kinds of things that can happen. Fitting elements of Christian worship with a dance service is one of the more creative areas of experimentation in alternative worship. In JOY we have tended to use dance at the end of the service because it offers us the best of both worlds.

NOTE

1. This idea was suggested to me by Crispin Fletcher.

15 · Pictures

A number of Christian writers have highlighted the importance of the visual arts in the worship of the Church. St John of Damascus said: "What the book is to the literate the image is to the illiterate."[1] This idea is quite widely repeated amongst the Fathers of the early Church. Today we are likely to talk about those people who are more comfortable with books and those who are more in touch with the visual world of video, film or TV. Young people are primarily "visually literate" and in tune with pictures and images. To ignore this particular aspect of youth culture in the development of alternative worship is to neglect one of the most stimulating and exciting areas of growth for the Church. But the visual arts are not a new area of Christian worship. In exploring the arts we are just re-learning lessons that the Church in earlier ages had grasped.

Every picture tells a story

For the medieval Christian, pictures and art were an ordinary and everyday part of their worship. Take for instance the statues which form part of the entrance to the Cathedral at Chartres. In the porch of this great Gothic church there are some remarkable figures carved in such a way that they seem to grow out of the stone. How anyone could make anything so beautiful and delicate out of stone I do not know.

But these figures are not there just for decoration. They were originally intended as an aid to worship. For the medieval worshipper these statues were lively and real signs of the presence of Christ in the world. Each is a key biblical figure who in some way heralded the coming of the Messiah. To represent this fact the medieval artist included in each sculpture a different symbol which speaks of the Good News of Jesus. Melchizedek the ancient priest holds the chalice which foretells the cup of wine in the Communion, Abraham who was prepared to sacrifice his son rests his hand on the head of Isaac, though we know that Jesus, God's Son, was not spared his sacrificial death. The statue of David the King shows him holding the crown of thorns which speaks of the King of Kings who died on a cross. Statues such as these at the entrance of the cathedral were there to introduce worshippers to the Gospel story as they came into the church, both welcoming them and preparing them for Jesus whom they will meet inside the church. Understanding these kinds of symbols in the art of a cathedral like Chartres was second nature to the thirteenth century Christian, but it is an ability which we have all but lost. We need guide books and experts to explain the symbolism in this sort of art.

The fact that previous generations were more in touch with the visual side of worship can be a source of inspiration and encouragement. In the first place we can begin to learn from them the way that art interacts with and inspires our praise for God. But this does not mean that we should try to turn all our services into lectures on classical Christian art. By looking at the art in places like Chartres we can be inspired to try things out in our own services. We should treat such art as a resource which can help us as we develop our own approach to visual images and worship.

The art of the Church

Youth culture is very creative in its use of the visual arts. In the average pop video hundreds of different images move about and change and whirl in fascinating ways. But it is not just in the use of video that youth culture leads the way. Young people are also the front-runners in the area of graphic design.

Magazines for young people are highly visual in their format. This is true of those for younger teenagers like Smash Hits as well as for the more sophisticated magazines for older youth like The Face. These magazines recognize how important the look of something is to most young people. But in church we pay very little attention to the look of our services.

The visual image of our worship has been inherited from an earlier age. The buildings were created before most of us were born. Different generations adapted these buildings to suit their own visual sensibilities. Stained glass windows, statues and monuments tell us of the artistic taste as well as the spirituality of the people who made them. These people had the confidence to use the art of their own day to express their Christian faith. They are an inspiration to young people today to use the modern media of film and video as an aid to worship as well as more traditional forms of creative expression.

Moving pictures

Traditional religious art is very static. A statue doesn't move. If you have a world-famous painting in your church you can't very easily swap it for something different when you get bored! But the modern visual world in which young people live is totally different. It is always on the move. In alternative worship the visual side of Christian worship is also very much on the move.

In JOY we have so far achieved this by using slide projectors. We have not yet used videos to any great extent, although if we could get easy access to the right kind of equipment we would. Slides are a much cheaper option. Most churches have a slide projector somewhere and slide film is easy to use and relatively inexpensive. With a large white sheet and a normal everyday slide projector we can achieve spectacular effects. A picture which is twenty feet high has an amazing impact. For this reason we always make our screens as big as we can.

Slides allow us to create a sequence of pictures which change throughout the service. We can create a visual environment for our worship which is infinitely variable. This is a quantum leap in the evolution of Christian worship. Suddenly the visual arts can become a responsive and interactive part of our worship. The look of a service is no longer static. The art of church worship moves! This factor alone will make alternative worship one of the most important and creative developments in church worship this century. Until now most services have consisted of a collection of words in a prayer book or of notes and words in a musical score. Alternative worship has broken through to another dimension. As well as our prayer books and our hymn books we will soon need worship picture books as well!

The rest of this chapter describes the JOY service which we prepared for the Communion on the Fringe at Greenbelt 1992. After a brief outline summary of each section of the service, it describes in more detail the pictures we used and how they interacted with the rest of the service.

Greenbelt Fringe Communion Service 1992

This service was specifically designed to present JOY to the people at Greenbelt as a church based on the Sacraments. Its theme was the Holy Communion.

We were anxious to convey the High Church elements that characterize JOY because in the context of Greenbelt this was what made us distinctive. The service explored the sacrifice that Jesus made on the Cross and how through taking Communion we are challenged to give our lives sacrificially to other people.

The layout

For this service we had five slide projectors and five screens all hanging at the front of the worship area. Directly in front of Screen 1 we set up the DJ and the record decks. In front of the DJ we placed the altar. We used six free standing ornate

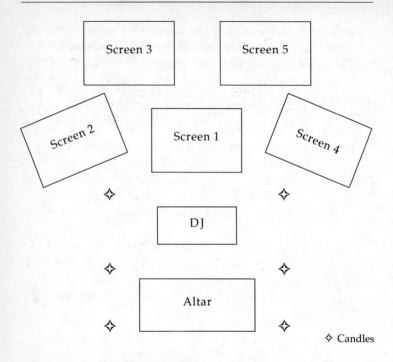

Diagram 1. Layout for the Communion service

candle sticks to frame the altar and the DJ. This layout for the
worship space set the visual scene for the theme of the service
– the centrality of the Communion – with the screens forming
a dramatic backdrop to the altar. The DJ and his decks and the
priest at the altar became a visual unity through the positioning
of the candle sticks. The candles symbolize the Holy Presence
of God, and both the DJ and the priest were seen to share in
this defined holy space. This emphasised the way youth culture
and the tradition of the Church were combined in our service.

Section 1: Rave

        SCREEN 1 Slogan: Prepare for Worship
                2 Crowd scene

4   Crowd scene
3   Elephant Stone
5   Elephant Stone

Dance music is playing when people arrive at the service. The visuals are also there for people to see right from the start. Their purpose is to set the scene for what is going to happen in the worship.

Screen 1 displays in large white letters on a black background the words Prepare for Worship. At this point nobody has said anything by way of introduction, but the message makes it clear that this is not a party, it is a worship service. On either side of the altar Screens 2 and 4 display the repeated image of a crowd of young people at a rave. The picture was taken by photographing a TV picture with a red filter. We find that pictures with a predominance of red have a very warm feel and help to create a "spiritual" atmosphere.

The rave scene is again echoed on Screens 3 and 5 by a psychedelic image taken from a Stone Roses album cover. This image and the crowd scene convey the message that in this service the world of the rave and the world of worship will be combined. The young people who come to the service find their own world reflected back to them in the symbolism of these pictures but this is contrasted with the command to worship.

Section 2: Welcome and Intro

SCREEN 1   Slogan: House of God
2   Crowd scene
4   Crowd scene
3   Rainbow Crucifix
5   Rainbow Crucifix

After people have danced for about fifteen minutes the leader stands up and welcomes everyone to the service. The picture on Screen 1 changes at this point to another slogan which reads

"The House of God". This prepares the way for the next song which has the same name, but it also conveys the message that this place has become special. In this service God will make his home among us. In this place we will share with him in his house. The word House is also used by young people for a form of music called "House Music". The phrase "The House of God" therefore has a dual significance.

Screens 2 and 4 remain the same but 3 and 5 have now changed to a picture of Christ on the Cross. It shows a repeated image of the crucified Jesus with the light coming from behind it and breaking out into rainbowlike rays. It speaks of the death of Christ reaching out into the world with its power to bring life. The service is about the death of Christ as it is portrayed in the Communion and already without actually saying anything we have started to direct people's thoughts along this road. Throughout the service we repeat the pictures in pairs on the screens. We use this technique because several pictures arranged symmetrically have added impact, while single images can be less powerful as well as being a bit distracting and confusing.

Section 3: Songs

SCREEN 1 World in Action Man
2 Song lyrics
4 Song lyrics
3 Michelangelo's Fingers
5 Michelangelo's Fingers

Repeating the song lyrics on Screens 2 and 4 mean that more people were able to see them in the crowded tent at Greenbelt. One of the songs is called Bridging the Gap. It speaks of God coming to us in the life of Jesus and how we in turn should reach out and bridge the gap which is between us and him.

The picture on Screens 3 and 5 echoes the idea with the well known image from Michelangelo's creation. God reaches out to bring life to Adam just as in our worship he comes to give us life. The image on Screen 1 is Leonardo Da Vinci's picture of the ideal man. When God meets us in worship we are made whole.

My wife Tess calls this the Renaissance section of the service because we are adopting works of art from that period of history into our worship. Using classical images from the art world is very handy because many of these pictures still have the power to move us. Some images may also be familiar to young people because they have been used in adverts or on TV, making them immediately more accessible. Leonardo's man was used by World in Action and Michelangelo's fingers feature in the titles of the South Bank Show. By using them in our worship we invest them with another layer of meaning. The familiarity of the picture causes people to ask questions about why it is being used at this point. This process may be conscious but more often it is not. Pictures often are experienced before they are thought about. In this way we take in the message of a picture very naturally without spending a lot of time analyzing it. Familiar images like Michelangelo's fingers regularly work this way. This is another good reason for using recognizable images from time to time to cash in on the fact that they already carry a significance. But when we see them in the context of worship the previous layer of meaning is transformed by a new spiritual message.

Section 4: Word: Meditation

SCREEN	1	Song lyrics
	2	Red Madonna
	4	Red Madonna
	3	Cloudburst
	5	Cloudburst

After reading 1 Corinthians 11: 23–29 where Paul talks about the Communion, two young people lead a meditation on these words, describing how God has challenged them to be sacrificial in their own lives. After each section of the meditation, which is said over the top of a backing track, we sing together the words displayed on Screen 1: "Father, be with us. Hear us, heal us."

To complement the quiet and meditative feel of this part of the service Screens 2 and 4 display the picture of the Madonna in Red. This image has an ethnic and rough feel to it but it conveys a sense of prayer and spiritual depth which we associate with Mary. Using the Madonna in this way also reinforces our aim of showing the traditional High Church side of JOY. But this is again contrasted with the techno-type backing track which accompanies the meditation. The red colour of this picture symbolizes an atmosphere of prayer, and Screens 3 and 5 reinforce this theme with the pictures of clouds.

Section 5: Communion

>   SCREEN 1 Blue Church Window
>   2 Liturgy words
>   4 Liturgy words
>   3 Psychedelic Madonnas
>   5 Psychedelic Madonnas

At this point in the service the priest in his traditional robes takes his place behind the altar to say the Eucharistic Prayer. The responses are displayed on Screens 3 and 5. In a normal JOY service we sing these sections with a live band supplying the music. At Greenbelt we decided to just say them because we wanted the Communion to flow with fewer interruptions and distractions.

Screen 1 displays a picture of a stained glass window with the figure of Christ outlined by streaming sunlight. This picture is the most popular image currently used at JOY. It speaks of Jesus the light of the world. The light seems to be pouring out of Jesus in a dramatic way. This image is directly behind the altar where we see the same outpouring repeated in the bread and wine of the Communion, and it is all framed by the psychedelic pictures of Madonnas. Again we are using a traditional image but the repetition of the image is one way of twisting it a little bit through the techniques of modern photography so that we see it a different way. Alternative worship recreates old images by combining them with the perspective of youth culture so that they appear fresh and more immediately relevant. This needs to be a continual process where we are all the time turning old symbols around so that we see them in a different light.

The priest says the words of the Communion and people are invited to take the bread and the wine while all the time dance music is playing, starting fairly low key but building in tempo and volume until it is very loud by the time everyone has received Communion. This adds to the drama – and Communion is dramatic and exciting because it is the place where God promises to meet us in the body and blood of Jesus.

Section 6: Songs

SCREEN	1	Spotty Church Window
	2	Song Lyrics
	4	Song Lyrics
	3	Blue Madonna
	5	Blue Madonna

We respond to receiving the Communion with a time of praise and thanksgiving. The song lyrics are on Screens 2 and 4 again so that people can join in. One of the songs pulls us back to the theme of Christ's sacrifice on the cross as seen in the Communion which inspires our own life of service for him: "Broken by, Broken by your love. Challenged by your love." We keep the general "churchy" feel of the service going with more Madonnas but this time they are in blue on Screens 3 and 5. On Screen 1 we have the picture of a church window which one of our JOY members likes because he says it always makes him feel spiritual. The service took place in a tent, but the image of the church interior reminds us that what we are doing is linked with the tradition of the rest of the Church.

Section 7: Rave

SCREEN	1	Baby and Water
	2	Slogan: Devotion
	4	Slogan: Freedom
	3	Big Fat Fish
	5	JOY Logo

The service ends by returning to a rave. People use this time to dance and generally let their hair down. For those of us who took part it is a time to relax and enjoy the fact that all the tension involved in doing the service is over. The slogans on Screens 2 and 4 however continue to highlight that this is part of the service. God gives us freedom but he also calls us to devotion. The Devotion slogan links up with the first song used in the rave, "I want to give you devotion" by Candy Stanton.

On screen we have a picture of a baby with water trickling down its face and this always gets a bit of a laugh. Using it at the end of the service reflects the lighter atmosphere that starts to set in after the Communion. It is also good to see a lovely human face smiling out at you at the end of the service!

Screen 3 shows a picture of a fish. This is a bit of a joke. A past member of JOY called Tamsin used this picture at the previous Greenbelt service. It's just a quirky touch that we like to put in from time to time and it reminds us of our history.

The JOY logo on Screen 5 is there to remind people of who we are. It's like a badge of identity.

Using five different pictures at this point provides a contrast to the more focused repeated ecclesiastical pictures used earlier in the service. We no longer need to make people concentrate on what is happening up front and a more stimulating visual environment echoes the informal feel of the rave.

This service was fairly complicated to produce. We had been

using slides in our worship for over a year and had some experience and expertise in the area. It is possible, however, to use two or three projectors and get some very good visual effects.

Working with pictures in worship is one of the most creative aspects of alternative worship in my experience and I would encourage any group to have a go! This service outline shows some of the ways that we are currently exploring this area, while other sections of this book e.g. the chapters on prayer and the elements of worship, refer to other ways in which we use pictures in our worship in JOY.

NOTE

1. Quoted in Jane Dillenberger, *Style in Contemporary Art*.

Additional note on pictures and copyright

Copyright of pictures is a more difficult area than music, where the Performing Rights Society handles copyright matters for composers. In general the copyright on a picture or a photograph is owned by the person who paid for the film in the camera. If you want to use an existing photograph or reproduce it in any way you need to ask the permission of that person. Needless to say this is not easy! If you have seen the picture in a magazine or a book the copyright is probably handled by one of the commercial agencies which supply pictures for publication. If this is the case you can usually get the address by contacting the publisher of the book or magazine where you first saw it. The chances are that the agency you then contact will charge a small fee for the use of the picture in your church service.

An easy way round this problem is to take original photographs yourself. If you take a picture of a painting or of a piece of architecture the copyright on that picture belongs to whoever bought the film in the camera. If that is you or your church then you only pay for the cost of the film.

Outro

Setting up an alternative worship service is a costly undertaking and yet I want to end this book by encouraging you to go ahead and do it. There is no doubt that young people given the right environment and encouragement can achieve amazing things. Indeed I would go as far as to say that they could even renew the Church!

I hope this book gives some clues as to how this weighty feat could come about. A vision which I know many people share is that God is moving in Britain. Our role it seems is to be willing to form creative relationships with young people. My experience has been that when we are willing to take the risk to build these kinds of friendships God blesses what we are doing in quite remarkable ways. The truth is that when youth culture is transformed by the Gospel it comes alive. When young people start to worship, the Spirit of God dances among them. The joy of the Lord is our strength.

If you want to know more about Oxford Youth Works and the training course which we run in Christian Youth Ministry please do get in touch. Our address is:

Oxford Youth Works
The Old Mission Hall
57B St Clements
Oxford
OX4 1AG

Bibliography

Athanasius, *On the Incarnation*, Mowbray 1944

Paul Avis, *Authority, Leadership and Conflict in the Church*, Mowbray 1992

John F. Baldwin, *City Church and Renewal*, The Pastoral Press 1991

Peter L. Berger and Thomas Luckmann, *The Social Construction of Reality*, Allen Lane 1966

Peter L. Berger, *The Social Reality of Religion*, Faber and Faber 1967

Jerome W. Berryman, *Godly Play*, Harper, San Francisco 1991

E. M. Blaiklock and A.C. Keys (translators), *The Little Flowers of St Francis*, Hodder and Stoughton 1985

Anthony Bloom, *Living Prayer*, Libra 1966

Leonardo Boff, *Sacraments of Life, Life of the Sacraments*, The Pastoral Press 1987

Springs, an adult faith-development programme, Geoffrey Chapman 1989

Walter Brueggemann, *Israel's Praise*, Fortress 1988

James Cone, *The Spirituals and the Blues*, Seabury 1972

Jean Corbon, *The Wellspring of Worship*, Paulist Press 1988

C.E.B. Cranfield, *The Service of God*, Epworth 1965

Robert Davidson, *Wisdom and Worship*, SCM 1990

J.G. Davies (ed), *A New Dictionary of Liturgy and Worship*, SCM 1986

J.G. Davies, *Worship and Mission*, SCM 1966

Jane Dillenberger, *Style in Contemporary Christian Art*, SCM 1986

John Dillenberger, *A Theology of Artistic Sensibilities*, SCM 1986

Kathy Galloway, *Imagining the Gospels*, SPCK 1988

Malcolm Grundy, *Evangelization Through the Adult Catechumenate*, Grove 1991

Gustavo Gutierrez, *We Drink from Our Own Wells*, SCM 1984

O. Hallesby, *Prayer*, IVP 1948

Bob Hopkins (ed), *Planting New Churches*, Eagle 1991

Gabe Huck, *Liturgy with Style and Grace*, Liturgy Training Publications 1984

Cheslyn Jones, Geoffrey Wainwright and Edward Yarnold (ed), *The Study of Liturgy*, SPCK 1978

Simon Law and Eric Lives, *Keep Music Legal*, Sea Dream Music (2nd ed) 1990

Margaret Miles, *The Image and Practice of Holiness*, SCM 1988

Henry Morgan (ed), *Approaches to Prayer*, SPCK 1991

Rudolf Otto, *The Idea of the Holy*, Oxford 1923

Marjorie Procter-Smith, *In Her Own Rite*, Abingdon 1990

Elaine Ramshaw, *Ritual and Pastoral Care*, Fortress 1987

Gail Ramshaw, *Christ in Sacred Speech*, Fortress 1986

Bruce Reed, *The Dynamics of Religion*, Darton Longman and Todd 1978

John Roberto (ed), *Access Guide to Liturgy and Worship*, Don Bosco, Multimedia 1990

Rosemary Radford Ruether, *Women-Church*, Harper and Row 1985

St Hilda Community, *Women Included*, SPCK 1991

Per-Olof Sjogren, *The Jesus Prayer*, SPCK 1975

Jon Michael Spencer, *Protest and Praise*, Fortress 1990

Katherine Spink, *A Universal Heart*, SPCK 1986

Paul Tudge, *Initiating Adults*, Grove 1988

Evelyn Underhill, *Worship*, Nisbet 1936

Pete Ward, *Youth Culture and the Gospel*, Marshall Pickering 1992

Michael Warren, *Faith Culture and the Worshipping Community*, Paulist Press 1989

Paul Willis, *Common Culture*, Open University 1990